MAKE MORE WORK LESS

The Guide to Unlocking Your Potential to Live and Work on Your Own Terms

Make More Work Less
The Guide to Unlocking Your Potential
to Live and Work on Your Own Terms

Published by
10-10-10 Publishing
1-9225 Leslie St.
Richmond Hill
Ontario, Canada
L4B 3H6

For information about special discounts for bulk purchases, please contact 10-10-10 Publishing at 1-888-504-6257.

Printed in the United States of America

ISBN-13:978-1508707837
ISBN-10: 1508707839

First Edition

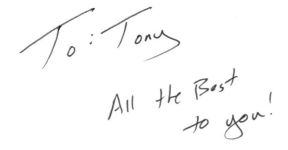

To: Tony

All the Best to you!

MAKE MORE WORK LESS

The Guide to Unlocking Your Potential to Live and Work on Your Own Terms

Unlock your Potential

on Today is the Day...

Fong Chua & Jessica Ng

- ABOUT THE AUTHORS -

Assurance Real Estate Acquisitions Inc. was brought together by the managing partners, Jessica Ng and Fong Chua, to bring to life their beliefs in adding value to people. This partnership specializes in uniting the right people, the right project and the right solution, all while adding value to all those involved, creating a win-win environment. Assurance Real Estate Acquisitions Inc. places great emphasis on relational capital, which is why we treat our clients and partners the same as our loved ones.

Starting out as engineers and winners of the Deal Makers Award, Fong and Jessica have the technical skills and attention to details to ensure that all projects are of value for all parties involved. We have many insider relationships with investors and agents, which allows us to have access to great deals first. Our philosophy is simple, we don't acquire properties unless they are below market value and we don't speculate on appreciation. When it comes to partnerships, three words describe our focus: loyalty, relationships and results. This is why we believe that partners should be for life and why we treat our partner's money even more conservatively than with our own.

Our Mission: To bring wealth, be it financial, knowledge or security, to all those who seek it. With our expertise and heart, it is our mission to impact as many people as we can by showing them how they can achieve more than they think.

This book is dedicated to:

Our parents, for their great lessons in life – ethics and the meaning of hard work. If not for these characteristics, we would not have had the foundation that got us to where we are today.

Our coaches, who inspire, motivate and believe in us. They remind us each day that we can achieve all our goals.

Each other, without the support and the dedication that we committed to our business and to each other, our ventures would not be possible.

- ACKNOWLEDGEMENTS -

We would like to acknowledge and thank all those involved with the publishing of this book for their hard work and care in putting this book together. We are absolutely thankful for their patience and time spent dealing with our requests.

Thank you to everyone that supported us in this venture: from writing, to editing (Louise Harris, LAST Research & Editing), to proofreading (Ryan Falkenberg), to cover design (Jong Chua, Just Creative Inc.), to photography (Wilson Wong, Everbrave Branding Group Ltd.), to guidance (Shawn Shewchuk, Coach) and assistance. Your assistance, support and motivation are deeply appreciated. We would also like to extend a heartfelt thank you to our circle of loving family, friends, clients and peers who have all been very supportive and encouraging to us.

Finally, we cannot thank Raymond Aaron enough for his friendship and phenomenal support during this adventure. Thank you Raymond for your belief in us and for writing the foreword to this book.

- CONTENTS -

- FOREWORD -

After having known and worked with Jessica and Fong for the past four years, I have seen great growth in both of them. They have taken the necessary steps to reach the goals many others have set for themselves, but never achieve. Their confidence is leaps and bounds ahead of where it used to be. In a short period of time, they have taken the knowledge that they have learned and applied it to their business and watched it grow.

Make More Work Less by Jessica and Fong is put together to help you understand that there is a lot more out there when it comes to preparing for your financial future; that you can Make More and Work Less, achieve more success and happiness in your life, if you open your mind and explore different vehicles and opportunities both traditional or nontraditional. We are in an era where the current concept of retirement is no longer acceptable. By looking at a few simple concepts and applying them to your life, you too can be set up for financial success and Make More and Work Less.

The values of relationship, caring and doing the right things are needed in both family and business today, and the authors would argue that without them, business is looking at an inescapable downfall. This book will encourage you to allow yourself to challenge your beliefs, find your values, guide your life accordingly and learn to be yourself as you venture into greater and newer opportunities that you have never thought of before today. While doing so, you will set up a financial future that allows you to take control of your life and also question things that you once thought to be 'normal.' By following just one or two of the concepts illustrated in this book, you will immediately change your future financial outlook and reduce a lot of stress, frustration, tension and above all, give you peace of mind.

The wisdom illustrated within the pages of this book will lead you to find new strengths and confidence and ultimately you will find great success in your financial future.

In this book:

- You will explore different strategies and concepts that will allow you to plan for your financial future.

- You will find the connection between beliefs, values, actions and outcomes that reinforce each other.

You will see that, as you hone your skills at questioning traditional beliefs, that many new opportunities will be open to you that will empower you to become more than you ever thought you could be and, in turn, live the life you always wanted to live.

Get ready to explore new methods to planning for a great financial future. Prepare yourself for change and success as you will see how easy it is to unlock your potential to live and work on your own terms!

Raymond Aaron
Author of eight books and co-author of the #1 Canadian Bestseller *Chicken Soup for the Canadian Soul™* and New York Times Top Ten Bestseller *Chicken Soup for the Parent's Soul™*.

- INTRODUCTION -

Long ago, Fong and I had gone to our first real estate event. We were excited to attend our first three-day event to learn what we needed to do to start on our path to financial freedom via real estate. We dreamt about how we would no longer have to worry about losing our engineering jobs should the oil and gas industry plummet; about how we can help our families, especially the ones overseas or those that aren't well off; and how we can finally make a bigger and better impact on our community. Things were going to be great!

During the three-day course, we had learned so much. We realized there was still so much we needed to know to get us to where we wanted to be. We had no idea that there was so much to real estate. We knew we needed more education to get us where we wanted to be. To help our families, friends and community and to live life on our own terms, not what our bosses tell us to do. We were scared out of our minds. We had just signed up for what we felt was a HUGE expense to learn the advanced techniques of real estate investing. It didn't matter though, our dreams and desires told us it was the right thing to do.

As we continued to learn about real estate over the years, we have now reached a level where we are comfortable with finding, maintaining and most of all, profiting from cashflowing properties. Looking back, we were SHOCKED to see how much time and money we spent on courses and books. If only we had a book that told us everything we should be doing to get good cashflow properties. Just one book, instead of the multiple books we had to read to be where we are today.

Throughout this time period of learning real estate, we have also networked and built great relationships with people in other industries. Getting to know what they do, we quickly realized that simply building a real estate portfolio is not enough. We realized that we must diversify and hedge our efforts into different vehicles of varying risks so that we have the financial future that we would like and to Make More and Work Less.

Through this book, we will illustrate how today's concept of retirement is no longer relevant. You can no longer just work hard your entire life in a "stable" job hoping that your employers or the investment funds from the bank will take care of you during your later years. People are living longer and cost of living is increasing. Therefore, we have realized that, if we did not set our financial future up to Make More as we Work Less, we would soon be in trouble.

After endless products, courses, seminars and information sessions, we believe that we have set ourselves up to be financially sound for the future. However, talking to many family and friends, we were taken aback about how little they knew about what is out there and what they may potentially be facing if they do not structure something soon.

Shocked at how little time people spend thinking about their financial future, we decided that we would like to simplify what we have learned and implemented in our lives and share it with our family, friends and all those who want to know more. In this book, we will discuss our four Pillars of Financial Foundation that will provide us with the freedom and comfort in our later years, whether or not we decide to retire.

Although this is but an introduction to the concepts that are being presented, we hope that it will open your mind to question current status quo investments and mindsets. We hope that it will encourage you to explore other nontraditional vehicles of financial support, instead of following the banking institutions and the governments.

We want to provide our valued readers a comprehensive guide to unlocking your potential to live and work on your own terms. We sincerely hope to help you achieve your dreams without having to spend the same amount of time and money that we have spent. It is our desire also that you will use your new skills to help your community and those in it. As Napoleon Hill put it, "It is literally true that you can succeed best and quickest by helping others succeed." Now, let's get into the keys of the book!

Thank you and enjoy!

Chapter - 1 -

Think More, Make More

"Make More and Work Less," isn't that what we all want to do? Unfortunately, too many people out there think that to Make More money, they must work more. They do not understand that until they actually THINK they can Make More and Work Less, that they will not do so. The mind will be so closed off from opportunities and possibilities of being able to Make More and Work Less, that they miss it all when the opportunities come to them. The purpose of this chapter is to show you how important your mindset is before you can Make More and Work Less. We will then illustrate, to you, why it is becoming more and more important in our society that you must Make More and Work Less as our retirement concept is misaligned. Furthermore, we will explore different vehicles that may help you to Make More and Work Less. And finally, how important it is to take action and build a great team to support you along the way. We hope that we can open your mind to new and different, nontraditional ways of planning and structuring your financial future so that you can truly Make More and Work Less.

Mind Set

Have you heard of the saying "You are what you eat"? Something less commonly heard is, "You are what you think." Henry Ford once said "Whether you think you can, or you think you can't -- you're right." Why then, do people not think more about success and opportunity? We have found that the reason there aren't more optimists is because, by nature, humans have been trained to see and think about the bad stuff. Have you ever noticed that the newspaper and news on TV thrives on informing us about the bad news that has happened in the world? People just don't respond to happy news the same way, so the media keeps informing us about the bad news. The more we hear about the bad news, the more we look for it. How can we stop ourselves from having this mindset? It all starts from within us. Granted, it's not easy to do. We have tried many things to keep us from being negative people. The good news, though, is that there are things we can do to help make ourselves become more positive people. The more effort you put into being positive, the easier it becomes. Being positive is somewhat like exercising a muscle. The more we exercise it, the stronger it is. By being more positive people, we will start seeing all the opportunities that are there rather than the obstacles that are there.

To help us remember to remain positive and open to opportunities rather than to fixate on negativity and obstacles, we have created an acronym: CAP

C: Confidence
A: Attitude
P: Persistence

Let's explore these a little more closely now.

Confidence

Sometimes, confidence trips us all. We find out the skills we are lacking and put in an effort to learning them, but then we start doubting ourselves. Can I really do this? What if I do it wrong? What if I don't know enough?

As with everything, you build confidence by doing it. You learn the skills, practice it and apply it. To help you understand how we build confidence, we will explain the four levels that we all go through when developing confidence. The first level is unconscious incompetence, the second is conscious incompetence, the third level is conscious competence and the last level is unconscious competence.

1 – Unconscious Incompetence
2 – Conscious Incompetence
3 – Conscious Competence
4 – Unconscious Competence

As an example, let's examine how we learned to drive. As we were growing up, we didn't know a thing about driving. It is just some magical thing that adults do. That's unconscious incompetence. Another way of putting this is you don't know what you don't know.

As we grow up, we realize that we could learn to drive too! It's not just something adults do, but something we can do as well, but we just don't know how. Now, we have reached the second level of conscious incompetence. We know what we don't know, but we don't know how to do it yet. This is why practice is so important.

In this example, most of us would go and get our learner's permit and take some driving lessons, and soon, we will get our license. Now, we have learned the skills we need to drive and have reached the third level of conscious competence. We still need to think about how to drive properly, but we have the necessary skills required to drive.

Finally, as we continue to apply our skills and keep driving, it will become so second nature that our bodies just know what to do. We no longer have to think "Don't forget to signal, if I turn right, I need to push the lever on the left hand side upwards." This level is unconscious competence. We just do it.

Once we are competent, we need to stop doubting ourselves and simply trust that we are able to do it. You didn't give up on driving just because you weren't sure of yourself did you? We hope you had just kept practicing until you were more comfortable. Anything we do in life is like that. Just as you trust that you can drive, you should trust in your abilities to learn the skills you need and apply it.

Attitude

Even if we were confident, we will need more than just that to help our mindset. We must have a good attitude. You might be asking yourself, how do I get that? The key is in your thoughts. As we have mentioned earlier, the more you exercise thinking positively, the easier it will get. But how do we even start thinking positively in the first place? It is all in your attitude and how you think about incidents.

Before we continue, we want to tell you a little story:

> *John and Mary were heading to the ski slope one weekend, but the road was blocked. They were really angry and upset because it was their last weekend to go skiing together for that season. With no way to reach the slope, they had to go home. On Monday, they picked up the newspaper and on the front page was a story about an avalanche with five people still missing. John and Mary realized that it was the same slope they were planning on going to visit. At this moment, they were so grateful for the roadblock that caused them to stay home and be safe.*

When you read that story, did you feel the same way as John and Mary? Most of us would. We would be mad at a situation that we felt inconvenienced us, and then, when something happens, our thoughts and attitude would change.

The fact is that John and Mary weren't able to go skiing. One moment, they were upset, and at another moment, they were grateful. Why not just skip the rollercoaster emotion and look for the good in what we may think is a bad situation at the time? By doing so, you could possibly see a hidden opportunity when most people would only see an obstacle.

Persistence

When you were young, do you remember learning to walk? Even if you don't, you know what the process is right? As a child, you started crawling, then you would stand with some support and as your legs grew stronger, you were able to stand without support. Finally, you would try to walk. Chances are high that the first few times you tried to walk, you stumbled and fell. Maybe you cried, maybe you didn't. Either way, you would try again and again to walk. Your parents or guardians would encourage you to do it and cheer you on.

Sometimes you might just want to give up, but with so many people cheering you on, you would try again and again. Finally, with enough practice and persistence, you unlocked the keys to walking. Now, walking is so second nature to you that you don't even have to tell yourself, "put your left foot out, step down, transfer your weight over to the left foot and bring your right foot forward." No, you can now walk without thinking.

Now that we are older, we won't necessarily have such a large fan base cheering us on to walk. This is why our attitude and our confidence are so important. Even so, there are times when we just want to give up. Things have gotten hard and things might not be going well. This is why we need persistence.

A key point we want to unlock at this point is what we call your "why." Why are you working on this goal? Why is this so important to you? Why keep working on it when it's so hard? Why, why, why. This is what will keep driving you on when things are getting you down and your attitude and confidence in yourself are no longer enough. If your why doesn't make you cry, keep working on finding it.

Your why becomes your mission and is the foundation of what you are building. If your foundation is weak, then what you are building will crumble in a matter of time. If your foundation is strong, no matter what wind or hardship is blowing on you, you hold the key to rebuilding because your foundation is still there.

So to start having a good mindset that looks for opportunity rather than obstacles, remember the acronym CAP: Confidence, Attitude and Persistence. Always believe in yourself, think positively about yourself and most of all: trust in your mission.

You might now be thinking, sure I can do those things, but how? To help aid you in that, we present two ideas: Vision board and Mind feeding.

Vision Board

Vision board is a presentation with pictures and words on it to help you visualize your goals. It should be placed some place visible to you daily as a reminder for yourself. Since you have picked up this book, we will assume that part of your goal is to Make More and Work Less. However, that is not the only thing in which vision boards are all about. Remember how we talked about your why? Your vision board should have that too. When times are hard, look at your vision board to give yourself the strength to go on. Now, what goes on a vision board? Good categories and questions to think about are:

- Family/Friends
    - Where do you see yourself with your family and friends?
    - Are there certain things you want to accomplish with them?
    - Who are the people you care about most?

- Financial
    - Where do you see yourself financially?
    - How many cashflowing properties do you see yourself owning?
    - Are there charities or causes that you want to support?

- Fun
    - Where do you want to go?
    - What do you want to have?
    - What do you want to do?

- Mental
  - Are there things you wish to learn?
  - What are some things you want to do to keep your mind active?
  - What new skills do you want to possess?

- Physical
  - Where do you see yourself physically and health wise?
  - Are there things you see yourself doing that you can't do now?
  - What foods should you want to eat?
  - Do you want to lose or gain weight?

- Spiritual
  - Are there places you want to travel to rejuvenate your spirit?
  - What are things you want to accomplish to keep your spirits high?

Each vision board is unique to the person. Some categories may not apply to you while other categories might not apply to others. Feel free to explore the possibilities of your vision board and to make it something you believe in yourself.

The more you see it, the more your mind will be "looking" for opportunities that bring those items to you. Instead of thinking that the items are dreams or farfetched goals, your mind will slowly believe that you already are in possession of the items in your vision board.

A great story about a powerful vision is that of Canadian Comedian and Actor Jim Carrey.

"I wrote myself a check for $10 million dollars for acting services rendered and dated it Thanksgiving 1995. I put it in my wallet and it deteriorated. And then, just before Thanksgiving 1995, I found I was going to make $10 million dollars for *Dumb and Dumber*. I put that check in the casket with my father because it was our dream together."

Mr. Carrey wrote himself a check, a vision of 10 million dollars. Seeing that vision every day, he was able to pick up opportunity after opportunity until one day, the vision was fulfilled.

Mind feed

Mind feed means feeding your brain with positive and stimulating things. Instead of watching TV and listening to the radio, consider reading or listening to a business book. There are many books and audio books out there that can uplift our spirit and remind us of our why. There are also many books and audio books out there that can enhance or teach us new skills. What do you let in your mind?

Ever hear people say: "Boy! Am I having a bad day..." or "Gee, nothing seems to be going my way today." Some of the things are happening all the time but never seemed to bother them before that day. The moment a person deems something is negative, awful or bad luck; their brains now are attracting everything else that can be interpreted as bad luck. They have concluded at the beginning of the day that they are having a bad day. Hence, mentally, they are looking for all the negative things around them to happen to fulfill the notion of a bad day. It is this aspect that makes mind feeding important. If you feed your mind with inspiration, motivation and information that will enrich your mind then you will live each and every day feeling inspired, motivated and attracting the feelings and opportunities that you have been feeding your mind. At a minimum, we should all be mind feeding every day for 30 minutes to an hour first thing in the morning. What better way to start the day than feeding your mind with riches?

Most people think garbage in means garbage out. Nido Qubein told us otherwise. He told us that when garbage gets in your mind, it doesn't just stay it gets pregnant and gives birth to triplets! So be careful what you let in your mind. Be selective about it and ensure that it supports the goals you have set for yourself on your vision board.

Mindset is a very important part to our road to success and in itself can be a very large topic. A great book on mindset that we highly recommend is *Change your Mind Change your Results – #1 Proven Success Strategies* by Shawn Shewchuk. We had the privilege of working with Mr. Shewchuk and can say without a doubt that his book and his teachings have changed our mindsets to seek opportunities, results and success. Feel free to contact us for more information.

A list of good books and audiobooks for mind feeding has been included at the end of this book as a reference for you. So let's keep in our minds Make More and Work Less!

Think SUCCESS and BE SUCCESSFUL!

Chapter - 2 -

Follow Less, Make More

Many ideas today were grandfathered from when they were created. However, because of how human nature is, we generally do not question why we do things or try to understand the reasoning behind doing them. We just do them.

For example, school is still the same as it has always been. We go to school from September to June and get two months of summer holidays in July and August. Do we ever ask why? Well, the months that we are in school coincide with the time farmers are not in the fields. The fall season is harvest season. They maintain it throughout the winter. They seed in the spring. They need helpers to work the fields in the summer. However, our society now should not be governed by the schedule of farming. We do not question why. We just do it because it has always been that way.

Retirement Should Be Retired

We would like people to start questioning the whole concept of retirement! Why is that what everyone wants? Why is retirement something that is fixated in our brains for a certain age? Why do we need to retire? When looking at these questions, more questions arise: where and why did the concept of retirement come from? Why is it not working today? And what should we do to avoid the pitfalls of retirement?

What is Retirement?

Let's start off by looking at the word retirement. When we look at the word retirement, we see the word retire. When we retire for the evening, it means we're done for the day.

We're going to sleep. Retirement means we are done all the hard work in life, time to go to take our long sleep. With that we ask, "If we love what we are doing, why do we need to be done with it?"

History Lesson

The concept of retirement comes from Germany in the 1890s. At that time, leaders in business needed a way to train young workers the skills the older workers held and to create vacancies for the younger workers. Life expectancy was 50 years old. The retirement age was set at 65, long past average life expectancy. If someone was still alive at age 65, the leaders would say, "Hey you know what? Thanks for all your years of service. Now, we are going to take care of you. We're going to look after you for whatever remaining years you have." A job then was created for the new worker.

Well that age of 65 has shifted forward in time, but it hasn't actually expanded any longer. We're living longer. The whole world and the whole environment have changed, yet, we're still working on this outdated model. So it doesn't seem rational that that's what's happening. For people to actually do that and live a comfortable life, they need to have savings in place and some protection on that savings, so that it's not just going to get wiped out by some mortgage crisis from another country.

Why is Retirement Not Working

Based on the entire concept of why retirement began, we can already see why the concept doesn't really apply to society today with life expectancies of 85, 90 and even 100 plus!

It is pretty typical for us all to think that we go to school, graduate, get a job, move up the corporate ladder, get raises, continue to work for 40 years from age 20-25 to 60-65 and then retire and live another 20 years. To that we ask, "Why do we want to retire if we love what we are doing? Why do we want to live with less than what we have now?" Times have changed and people are living longer and longer. In 1890s, it was 50; then it was 70; a few years ago it was 80; now, it's 85 and more and more stories come and go about people living to 100 or 115.

We Are Living Longer

If your plan was to work till you are 65, what if you live healthily to the age of 95? Where are you going to get that extra 10 years of retirement fund? A few years ago, the magic number for retirement was $1 million in your account so that you can live on $60 thousand a year, after tax dollars till the age of 85. With people living longer that number is now $1.5 million to $2 million. That doesn't even allow for inflation! As we look at what society is promoting, what banks are offering and what we hear from family and friends, we get more frustrated at what people don't know, what we didn't know and was not told!

It Doesn't Add Up!

We decided to look at the numbers a little closer. You will see a table illustrating this example in the following pages. To download a copy for easier viewing, go to our website, www.makemoreworklessbook.com. Now, let's assume that you have your money in an investment fund. A government supported fund that will give a return of 5 percent compounded annually. Let's assume 30 percent of your gross income goes to taxes and that you want to have $60 thousand a year after tax dollars starting at the age of 65. Based on these assumptions, you will need to consistently deposit $10,200 each year starting at the age of 25, so that you can have enough funds ($86,000 per year gross to have $60,000 after tax dollars, assuming 30% tax) to live to the age of 90. With the recent markets, how many people can honestly say that they have made 5 percent compounded annually on their plans? Is that realistic? Or is 2.5 percent more likely to happen? At 2.5 percent, you will need to deposit $24,000 a year if the same assumptions are maintained. Now we don't know about you, but we were not getting 2.5 percent on our government funds. In fact, we would be happy if it was not negative! Even if it was at 5 percent, we haven't accounted for inflation and we also have not been saving $10,200 each year since we were 25. Does this really sound like you can retire early and work less? It sounds more like working 40 years is nowhere near enough!

MAKE MORE WORK LESS

2.5% versus 5.0% Compounded Annually

Year	Age	Withdraw	Deposit at end of year (for 2.5% case)	Account Amount at end of year (for 2.5% case)	Deposit at end of year (for 5.0% case)	Account Amount at end of year (for 5.0% case)
1	25	$ -	$ 24,000.00	$ 24,000.00	$ 10,200.00	$ 10,200.00
2	26	$ -	$ 24,000.00	$ 48,600.00	$ 10,200.00	$ 20,910.00
3	27	$ -	$ 24,000.00	$ 73,815.00	$ 10,200.00	$ 32,155.50
4	28	$ -	$ 24,000.00	$ 99,660.38	$ 10,200.00	$ 43,963.28
5	29	$ -	$ 24,000.00	$ 126,151.88	$ 10,200.00	$ 56,361.44
6	30	$ -	$ 24,000.00	$ 153,305.68	$ 10,200.00	$ 69,379.51
7	31	$ -	$ 24,000.00	$ 181,138.32	$ 10,200.00	$ 83,048.49
8	32	$ -	$ 24,000.00	$ 209,666.78	$ 10,200.00	$ 97,400.91
9	33	$ -	$ 24,000.00	$ 238,908.45	$ 10,200.00	$ 112,470.96
10	34	$ -	$ 24,000.00	$ 268,881.16	$ 10,200.00	$ 128,294.50
11	35	$ -	$ 24,000.00	$ 299,603.19	$ 10,200.00	$ 144,909.23
12	36	$ -	$ 24,000.00	$ 331,093.27	$ 10,200.00	$ 162,354.69
13	37	$ -	$ 24,000.00	$ 363,370.60	$ 10,200.00	$ 180,672.43
14	38	$ -	$ 24,000.00	$ 396,454.87	$ 10,200.00	$ 199,906.05
15	39	$ -	$ 24,000.00	$ 430,366.24	$ 10,200.00	$ 220,101.35
16	40	$ -	$ 24,000.00	$ 465,125.40	$ 10,200.00	$ 241,306.42
17	41	$ -	$ 24,000.00	$ 500,753.53	$ 10,200.00	$ 263,571.74
18	42	$ -	$ 24,000.00	$ 537,272.37	$ 10,200.00	$ 286,950.32
19	43	$ -	$ 24,000.00	$ 574,704.18	$ 10,200.00	$ 311,497.84
20	44	$ -	$ 24,000.00	$ 613,071.78	$ 10,200.00	$ 337,272.73
21	45	$ -	$ 24,000.00	$ 652,398.58	$ 10,200.00	$ 364,336.37
22	46	$ -	$ 24,000.00	$ 692,708.54	$ 10,200.00	$ 392,753.19
23	47	$ -	$ 24,000.00	$ 734,026.26	$ 10,200.00	$ 422,590.85
24	48	$ -	$ 24,000.00	$ 776,376.91	$ 10,200.00	$ 453,920.39
25	49	$ -	$ 24,000.00	$ 819,786.33	$ 10,200.00	$ 486,816.41
26	50	$ -	$ 24,000.00	$ 864,280.99	$ 10,200.00	$ 521,357.23
27	51	$ -	$ 24,000.00	$ 909,888.02	$ 10,200.00	$ 557,625.09
28	52	$ -	$ 24,000.00	$ 956,635.22	$ 10,200.00	$ 595,706.34
29	53	$ -	$ 24,000.00	$ 1,004,551.10	$ 10,200.00	$ 635,691.66
30	54	$ -	$ 24,000.00	$ 1,053,664.88	$ 10,200.00	$ 677,676.24
31	55	$ -	$ 24,000.00	$ 1,104,006.50	$ 10,200.00	$ 721,760.06
32	56	$ -	$ 24,000.00	$ 1,155,606.66	$ 10,200.00	$ 768,048.06
33	57	$ -	$ 24,000.00	$ 1,208,496.83	$ 10,200.00	$ 816,650.46
34	58	$ -	$ 24,000.00	$ 1,262,709.25	$ 10,200.00	$ 867,682.99
35	59	$ -	$ 24,000.00	$ 1,318,276.98	$ 10,200.00	$ 921,267.13
36	60	$ -	$ 24,000.00	$ 1,375,233.90	$ 10,200.00	$ 977,530.49
37	61	$ -	$ 24,000.00	$ 1,433,614.75	$ 10,200.00	$ 1,036,607.02
38	62	$ -	$ 24,000.00	$ 1,493,455.12	$ 10,200.00	$ 1,098,637.37
39	63	$ -	$ 24,000.00	$ 1,554,791.50	$ 10,200.00	$ 1,163,769.24
40	64	$ -	$ 24,000.00	$ 1,617,661.28	$ 10,200.00	$ 1,232,157.70
41	65	$ 86,000.00	$ -	$ 1,572,102.82	$ -	$ 1,207,765.58
42	66	$ 86,000.00	$ -	$ 1,525,405.39	$ -	$ 1,182,153.86
43	67	$ 86,000.00	$ -	$ 1,477,540.52	$ -	$ 1,155,261.55
44	68	$ 86,000.00	$ -	$ 1,428,479.04	$ -	$ 1,127,024.63
45	69	$ 86,000.00	$ -	$ 1,378,191.01	$ -	$ 1,097,375.86
46	70	$ 86,000.00	$ -	$ 1,326,645.79	$ -	$ 1,066,244.66
47	71	$ 86,000.00	$ -	$ 1,273,811.93	$ -	$ 1,033,556.89
48	72	$ 86,000.00	$ -	$ 1,219,657.23	$ -	$ 999,234.73
49	73	$ 86,000.00	$ -	$ 1,164,148.66	$ -	$ 963,196.47
50	74	$ 86,000.00	$ -	$ 1,107,252.38	$ -	$ 925,356.29
51	75	$ 86,000.00	$ -	$ 1,048,933.69	$ -	$ 885,624.11
52	76	$ 86,000.00	$ -	$ 989,157.03	$ -	$ 843,905.31
53	77	$ 86,000.00	$ -	$ 927,885.95	$ -	$ 800,100.58
54	78	$ 86,000.00	$ -	$ 865,083.10	$ -	$ 754,105.61
55	79	$ 86,000.00	$ -	$ 800,710.18	$ -	$ 705,810.89
56	80	$ 86,000.00	$ -	$ 734,727.93	$ -	$ 655,101.43
57	81	$ 86,000.00	$ -	$ 667,096.13	$ -	$ 601,856.51
58	82	$ 86,000.00	$ -	$ 597,773.54	$ -	$ 545,949.33
59	83	$ 86,000.00	$ -	$ 526,717.87	$ -	$ 487,246.80
60	84	$ 86,000.00	$ -	$ 453,885.82	$ -	$ 425,609.14
61	85	$ 86,000.00	$ -	$ 379,232.97	$ -	$ 360,889.59
62	86	$ 86,000.00	$ -	$ 302,713.79	$ -	$ 292,934.07
63	87	$ 86,000.00	$ -	$ 224,281.64	$ -	$ 221,580.78
64	88	$ 86,000.00	$ -	$ 143,888.68	$ -	$ 146,659.82
65	89	$ 86,000.00	$ -	$ 61,485.89	$ -	$ 67,992.81
66	90	$ 86,000.00		-$ 22,976.96		-$ 14,607.55

NOTES:
1. Assume that 30% of gross income goes towards taxes. In order to take $60,000/year, $86,000 must be withdrawn.
2. You save up at age 25 and start your investment account at the end of age 25. No interest has accumulated yet.
3. Total saved over 40 years (age 25 to 64): 2.5% case = $960,000. 5.0% case = $408,000.
4. Retire at age 65 and start withdrawing to receive $60,000 after taxes.
5. Retirement amount available at age 65: 2.5% case = $1,572,102. 5.0% case = $1,207,765.
6. By age 90, there will be no money left.

Fig. 2-1. Compound Comparison 2.5% VS. 5%

That's Not All! Sneaky Thing about Averages!

We all know that things go up and down, but has anyone looked carefully at percentages? If something drops 50 percent you need to GAIN 100 percent to make up for that 50 percent loss. So if you want to come out ahead, you need to gain even more than 100 percent! For example, if we had $100 and in Year No. 1 we had a good year of 100 percent return, that means we now have $200! Unfortunately, Year No. 2 did not go so well and it lost 50 percent, so we now have $100. Year No. 3 was up another 100 percent. So we are once again riding high at $200, until a sad Year No. 4 where we lost another 50 percent, right back down to $100. So how much did you make? Nothing! BUT...your average gain over the last four years is a whopping 25 percent!

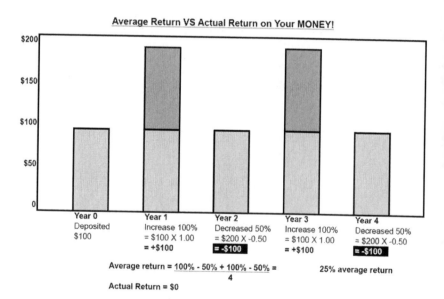

Fig. 2-2. Average VS. Actual ROI

Looking at these numbers really infuriated us and led us to ask more questions! How is this possible? Why are we not being told otherwise? Why is this concept of retirement so sought after when percentages are not really true? And what am I going to do? I'm five years late on my savings!

What to Do? What to Do?!

So what are we to do? Please do not get us wrong. We are not selling anything and not trying to scare anyone here. We are angry about what we didn't know and wish desperately that someone could have told us earlier.

Our parents are by no means lacking in intelligence, they just did what they thought was right at the time and hence taught us to do the same. But times have changed. That concept of saving for retirement doesn't work anymore. What we want to stress to everyone is keep an open mind and seek advice from one, two or three different advisers. You may have someone already doing a superb job, great, but could it be better?

Get a Second Opinion Outside the System

Ask experts outside the influence of banks and government what they think. Seek other nontraditional vehicles of savings and investing, such as life insurance, land banking, exempt markets, commodities and real estate. Talk to professional financial experts and see what their view points are. Everyone has their "thing." It doesn't hurt to hear what those opinions are and decide for yourself if they are a good fit for you instead of never, ever knowing about them.

Be Open Minded

Read that leaflet or brochure on investing or that flyer in the mail before discarding it. Some of the safest investments may actually be the least talked about and those that are most promoted may actually be the most risky. Allow yourself to live life on your own terms. If you love what you do, then logically you would never want to retire. Why would you? Getting paid to do what you love would be a dream! So if you are indeed doing something that you absolutely love, then GREAT! I'm sure you don't really think about retirement. But for those of you that do not love what you are doing, you may already be counting the days to retirement, why not put in that extra 10 percent of effort and start something new on the side, build it and eventually leave the job that you don't enjoy and do something that you love to do and get paid for it. If done correctly, that can ultimately be your retirement plan.

What Most People Are Doing Now

A lot of people understand that the numbers do not add up. They know that they need to do something with their money for them to have the life they want to live in the future. They understand the concept of "having your hard earned money work for you." However, what they are not knowledgeable in is how to do so. They will then go to the financial "experts" at the bank and ask them for advice. How is that different from you going into a hair salon and asking the stylist, "In your expert opinion, do you think I need a haircut and style?" Well of course you do!!

What Is Actually Happening

Banks WANT you to put money into their accounts so that they can lend more money out to other people. They put your money into low returning funds while making much greater returns on the money that you deposit. The financial expert makes money regardless if your "investment" makes money or loses money. Isn't it curious that a bank will not lend you money to buy their funds? Yet they would lend money to buy a house? Funds are susceptible to the market, they go up and they go down, and therefore, to appease their clients, banks will spice it up, giving the funds exciting names like Super Fund, BRIC Fund and Mortgage Fund, but really they just give you low returns in the long run if at all.

Stocks

Stocks are a great way to start investing your money. It requires a lot of time and education, but everything that is worth knowing is worth learning. If you put the time and effort into stocks, you can do better than any of the funds that the "experts" have recommended. Although the same can be said, if you do not spend the time and effort to learn about stocks and trading, things can go really wrong.

Concepts such as PUT options and CALL options are simple strategies that you can apply to your stock trading to get you very different results. However, many people do not have the time and/or the interest to look at numbers and charts and reports. Hence, they go to the bank experts in the first place. You have to understand that by doing so, you have no control over how stocks do. You do not have a say as to how the companies in that stock should work, who should be hired, or what products should be sold. Neither do the "experts" at the bank. They were hired and trained to sell you on a specific bond or fund and will get paid regardless of the performance of the investment.

Second Opinion

Instead of seeking the advice on how you should invest your money based on a biased opinion, why not seek other experts who have the same access to the funds the banks do and a world of other funds that the banks do not promote? Why not ask the experts who have studied all the funds and companies and businesses and not just that of a bank? There are many financial planners and experts who will work hard for your best interest. They are paid by the companies that take your investments, so you are not out of pocket. They know that if they do not perform, you will leave and therefore, will advise and recommend from a large arena of investments that is the best fit for you and your goals. Make sure you interview a few advisers or experts before you decide on which you want to work with. Ask good questions and get to know them as a person and decide whether or not you want to work with them for the long term.

By doing so, you are now taking a first step outside the traditional way in how you can actually Make More and Work Less.

If traditional methods are not working, find solutions outside of what everyone else is doing.

Chapter - 3 -

Be Insured, Make More

We understand that people have different tolerances for risks and different methods as to how they manage risk. Investing and topics about money are generally viewed very carefully and emotionally. It is something that is very dear to people. You work hard for that money and you would like it to be there when you need it. However, as we have indicated in the previous chapter, you must take some carefully managed risks if you want to Make More and Work Less!

Four Pillars of Financial Foundation

To manage risk we like to refer to our four pillars of financial foundation: Insurance, Land, Commodities and Real Estate. To us, stocks are out of our control and we are not experts on the subject. We do however, have professional financial advisers who look after a portion of our investments in funds and stocks. To create a strong foundation for our plan to Make More and Work Less, we have decided that we would like to place our money, time and education on our four pillars of financial foundation where they all have a different risk level to them, different return potential and most importantly something that we can control.

Say It Isn't So...REALLY?

The first pillar that we would like to discuss is the foundation of our plan, the rock that holds everything together. It is in our opinion the safest, least risky and most important pillar of our empire: Life Insurance.

The Common Stereotype of Life Insurance

We know. We know. "Boo life insurance." Unfortunately, we as a society frown upon life insurance. Not because of what its purpose is, but what it cannot do for us today. The common knowledge is that life insurance is only good when you are gone so that the people that you care about are looked after. However, many people do not understand the full value of life insurance and don't see the living benefits that life insurance can provide. To utilize life insurance as a life benefit, you must also be using the appropriate type of life insurance and have it structured properly so that your money is maximized to its fullest. Once you get it set up strategically, it will ultimately provide you the foundation to Make More and Work Less.

Types of Life Insurance

The whole concept of this book is to show you ways where you can Make More and Work Less. It is only logical to relate insurance similar to an investment. However, you soon will see that it is much more like a savings vehicle that grows instead of an investment that is subject to market trends.

Just like cars can have different brands, types and features. Insurance also has many different type of structures and features. It is how you set them up and how you utilize them that allow you to benefit from them like the wealthy do. Three main types of life insurance have their own branches of different versions and structures. They are: Term Life, Universal Life and Whole Life. Let's look at each one individually.

Term Life Insurance

The best way to look at term insurance is that it is like renting the benefits of insurance, similar to renting a house. When you rent a house, you pay your rent and you get the benefit of living there. If the property goes up in value, you have no connection to that increase. When your rental term is done, you will need to go find another place and you get nothing from the previous place or you renew at your current place at what may be a higher rent because the property value went up or because the rental market demands a higher rent. In the end, you have no vested interest in the property itself.

This is almost the same with term insurance. You pay a premium (rent) for the benefit of having a life insurance policy for a period of time (term). If anything happens to you during that time, your beneficiaries will be taken care of by the benefits that you have been renting. However, if nothing happens (which is what both you and the insurance company wants), then at the end of the term you get nothing from it. Now that your term is expired, you will need to renew the term at a higher cost due to you being older. Term insurance has its purposes and is fit for those who are seeking the short-term benefits and its low cost. However, from a long-term protection stand point, it doesn't make much sense.

Universal Life Insurance

Universal Life Insurance combines the concept of protecting your loved ones while also helping you prepare for the future. You may have heard some people say "buy term insurance and invest the difference." Universal Life

Insurance does this for you in one policy. It allows people to get into saving and investing for the future and also feel that they are providing the protection their family needs. However, as we know, term insurance is like renting and when the term has ended, the cost of the insurance is higher and therefore, less will be invested for the future. In addition, you end up investing in similar products that banks offer you. They are stocks, bonds and funds that: A) give you no control and B) are all subject to the highs and lows of the market. Therefore, you may not have saved as much as you thought, since you could lose a large amount during a poor market year.

If you think more carefully about the concept, why are you buying term insurance where you are betting that you will not live past the term date, yet investing for the future where you are hoping to live past the term date? In our opinion that seems a bit contradictory. In addition, insurance companies are here to make money and therefore they have everything calculated for term insurance knowing that you will likely not be cashing out before the term is done. In fact, only about 2 to 3 percent of term insurance is paid out!

Whole Life Insurance – The Best Kept Secret of the Rich

Following the analogy of properties, Whole Life Insurance and, in particular, Participating Dividend Paying Whole Life Insurance (PDPWLI) is like buying a property. When you buy a property you have a vested interest as to what happens to your property. If the property goes up in value you reap the benefits of that increase. You pay down the mortgage and build up equity in your property. After years of paying down the property, you now have the right to access the equity in your property. You can get a line of credit secured on your property. You can refinance the property and pull out some equity. What you do with the funds is up to you: go on vacation, buy another property, pay off debt, etc.

As long as you set up your whole life insurance the correct way, you too can do the same with the insurance as you would with a house, except with insurance you are not subject to any market trends like a house may be. You pay your premiums (mortgage) and by contract your cash value (equity) of your insurance policy must grow. Because of the structure of PDPWLI, if the insurance company makes money, you share in the profits. These profits will come back to you as dividends which you can take in cash, pay down your next year's premiums or purchase another block of whole life insurance. Unlike term insurance where you need to requalify each time you renew a term, with whole life you only need to qualify the first time and all future blocks of insurance is automatically approved. If each block of life insurance is by contract guaranteed to grow and each block of insurance brings back dividends, then the cash value will continue to grow. Your payments will always remain the same and your increases in cash value are locked in, never to be reduced. In the end, you also have the benefit of a growing death benefit with the additional blocks of life insurance that you are getting with the dividends that you can leave behind to protect your loved ones.

Similar to refinancing or getting a line of credit on your property to access the equity, you also can do so with the cash value of your policy. Again what you do with that money is up to you. You can pay off debts, invest it, purchase a car or even retire off it. The possibilities are endless. Now, if you borrow money from your property equity, does it affect the appreciation of the property itself? No. The same goes for your policy. Regardless of what you are borrowing from your policy, the dividends and cash values will continue to grow like it was all still there.

It is true that whole life is more costly than term, like renting versus mortgage payments but the benefits far outweigh the cost. What you put in it is what you get back with whole life. What you put into term, you get nothing back. If you put in more for whole life, your cash value grows faster. If you put in less, it grows slower and your death benefit is less. Similar to a loan on your property, you also have to pay back interest on the loan you make on your policy. However, the interest rates are generally much less than credit cards or other money lending institutions and less than potential investment returns. Hence, wouldn't it make sense to borrow from your policy to pay off high interest rate loans or utilize the funds to get great returns?

Since the increases are locked, what you put in it will be recovered and the system will never lose money, wouldn't you say that this is truly what savings is all about? It's not an investment. This concept has been around for decades and most people do not know about this. This is the concept that the wealthy are using. The more wealth they accumulate the more insurance they have. Large banking institutions buy large whole life policies on their CEOs, borrow from the cash value and lend the funds out to people who need to purchase homes. The banks and the wealthy are using this strategy to Make More and Work Less, why not you?

To download a copy of the following charts, for easier viewing, see www.makemoreworklessbook.com.

Death Benefit VS Cash Value VS Age of Policy Owner

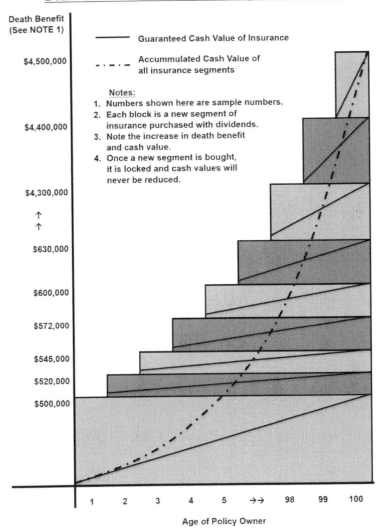

Death Benefit
(See NOTE 1)

—————— Guaranteed Cash Value of Insurance

$4,500,000

— · — · — Accummulated Cash Value of
all insurance segments

Notes:
1. Numbers shown here are sample numbers.
2. Each block is a new segment of
   insurance purchased with dividends.
3. Note the increase in death benefit
   and cash value.
4. Once a new segment is bought,
   it is locked and cash values will
   never be reduced.

$4,400,000

$4,300,000

$630,000

$600,000

$572,000

$545,000

$520,000

$500,000

1   2   3   4   5   →→   98   99   100

Age of Policy Owner

Fig. 3-1. Death Benefit VS. Cash Value VS. Age

Let's compare saving with Insurance VS What most are doing as mentioned in Chapter 2.

Life Insurance versus 5.0% Compounded Annually

Year	Age	Premiums (for Life Insurance case)	Cash Value (for Life Insurance case)	Growth in Cash Value (for Life Insurance case)	Withdrawal (from Life Insurance case)	Available Cash Value (from Life Insurance case)	Withdrawal (from 5.0% investment account)	Deposit at end of year (for 5.0% case)	Account Amount at end of year (for 5.0% case)
1	25	$ -	$ -	$ -	$ -	$ -	$ -	$ -	$ -
2	26	$ -	$ -	$ -	$ -	$ -	$ -	$ 10,200.00	$ 10,200.00
3	27	$ -	$ -	$ -	$ -	$ -	$ -	$ 10,200.00	$ 20,910.00
4	28	$ 11,545.00	$ -	$ -	$ -	$ -	$ -	$ 10,200.00	$ 32,155.50
5	29	$ 11,545.00	$ 5,954.94	$ 5,954.94	$ -	$ 5,954.94	$ -	$ 10,200.00	$ 43,963.28
6	30	$ 11,545.00	$ 14,752.46	$ 8,797.52	$ -	$ 14,752.46	$ -	$ 10,200.00	$ 56,361.44
7	31	$ 11,545.00	$ 25,519.00	$ 10,766.54	$ -	$ 25,519.00	$ -	$ 10,200.00	$ 69,379.51
8	32	$ 11,545.00	$ 38,652.00	$ 13,133.00	$ -	$ 38,652.00	$ -	$ 10,200.00	$ 83,048.49
9	33	$ 11,545.00	$ 52,380.00	$ 13,728.00	$ -	$ 52,380.00	$ -	$ 10,200.00	$ 97,400.91
10	34	$ 11,545.00	$ 66,053.00	$ 13,673.00	$ -	$ 66,053.00	$ -	$ 10,200.00	$ 112,470.96
11	35	$ 11,545.00	$ 80,360.00	$ 14,307.00	$ -	$ 80,360.00	$ -	$ 10,200.00	$ 128,294.50
12	36	$ 11,545.00	$ 96,638.00	$ 15,878.00	$ -	$ 96,638.00	$ -	$ 10,200.00	$ 144,909.23
13	37	$ 11,545.00	$ 113,159.00	$ 16,521.00	$ -	$ 113,159.00	$ -	$ 10,200.00	$ 162,354.69
14	38	$ 11,545.00	$ 130,609.00	$ 17,450.00	$ -	$ 130,609.00	$ -	$ 10,200.00	$ 180,672.43
15	39	$ 11,545.00	$ 148,447.00	$ 17,836.00	$ -	$ 148,447.00	$ -	$ 10,200.00	$ 199,906.05
16	40	$ 11,545.00	$ 167,719.00	$ 19,272.00	$ -	$ 167,719.00	$ -	$ 10,200.00	$ 220,101.35
17	41	$ 11,545.00	$ 187,845.00	$ 20,126.00	$ -	$ 167,845.00	$ -	$ 10,200.00	$ 241,306.42
18	42	$ 11,545.00	$ 209,257.00	$ 21,412.00	$ -	$ 209,257.00	$ -	$ 10,200.00	$ 263,571.74
19	43	$ 11,545.00	$ 232,019.00	$ 22,762.00	$ -	$ 232,019.00	$ -	$ 10,200.00	$ 286,950.32
20	44	$ 11,545.00	$ 255,298.00	$ 23,279.00	$ -	$ 255,298.00	$ -	$ 10,200.00	$ 311,497.84
21	45	$ 11,545.00	$ 280,147.00	$ 24,849.00	$ -	$ 280,147.00	$ -	$ 10,200.00	$ 337,272.73
22	46	$ 11,545.00	$ 306,650.00	$ 26,503.00	$ -	$ 306,650.00	$ -	$ 10,200.00	$ 364,336.37
23	47	$ 11,545.00	$ 334,916.00	$ 28,266.00	$ -	$ 334,916.00	$ -	$ 10,200.00	$ 392,753.19
24	48	$ -	$ 365,044.00	$ 30,128.00	$ -	$ 365,044.00	$ -	$ 10,200.00	$ 422,590.85
25	49	$ -	$ 388,101.00	$ 23,057.00	$ -	$ 388,101.00	$ -	$ 10,200.00	$ 453,920.39
26	50	$ -	$ 412,486.00	$ 24,385.00	$ -	$ 412,486.00	$ -	$ 10,200.00	$ 486,616.41
27	51	$ -	$ 438,274.00	$ 25,788.00	$ -	$ 438,274.00	$ -	$ 10,200.00	$ 521,357.23
28	52	$ -	$ 465,520.00	$ 27,246.00	$ -	$ 465,520.00	$ -	$ 10,200.00	$ 557,625.09
29	53	$ -	$ 494,302.00	$ 28,782.00	$ -	$ 494,302.00	$ -	$ 10,200.00	$ 595,706.34
30	54	$ -	$ 524,677.00	$ 30,375.00	$ -	$ 524,677.00	$ -	$ 10,200.00	$ 635,691.66
31	55	$ -	$ 556,749.00	$ 32,072.00	$ -	$ 556,749.00	$ -	$ 10,200.00	$ 677,676.24
32	56	$ -	$ 590,553.00	$ 33,804.00	$ -	$ 590,553.00	$ -	$ 10,200.00	$ 721,760.06
33	57	$ -	$ 626,172.00	$ 35,619.00	$ -	$ 626,172.00	$ -	$ 10,200.00	$ 768,048.06
34	58	$ -	$ 663,686.00	$ 37,514.00	$ -	$ 663,686.00	$ -	$ 10,200.00	$ 816,650.46
35	59	$ -	$ 703,146.00	$ 39,460.00	$ -	$ 703,146.00	$ -	$ 10,200.00	$ 867,682.99
36	60	$ -	$ 744,614.00	$ 41,468.00	$ -	$ 744,614.00	$ -	$ 10,200.00	$ 921,267.13
37	61	$ -	$ 788,169.00	$ 43,575.00	$ -	$ 788,169.00	$ -	$ 10,200.00	$ 977,530.49
38	62	$ -	$ 833,928.00	$ 45,759.00	$ -	$ 833,928.00	$ -	$ 10,200.00	$ 1,036,607.02
39	63	$ -	$ 881,895.00	$ 47,967.00	$ -	$ 881,895.00	$ -	$ 10,200.00	$ 1,098,637.37
40	64	$ -	$ 932,169.00	$ 50,274.00	$ -	$ 932,169.00	$ -	$ 10,200.00	$ 1,163,769.24
41	65	$ -	$ 984,831.00	$ 52,662.00	$ 60,000.00	$ 924,831.00	$ 86,000.00	$ -	$ 1,232,157.70
42	66	$ -	$ 1,038,927.00	$ 56,096.00	$ 60,000.00	$ 978,927.00	$ 86,000.00	$ -	$ 1,307,765.58
43	67	$ -	$ 1,097,528.00	$ 57,601.00	$ 60,000.00	$ 1,037,528.00	$ 86,000.00	$ -	$ 1,182,153.86
44	68	$ -	$ 1,157,712.00	$ 60,184.00	$ 60,000.00	$ 1,097,712.00	$ 86,000.00	$ -	$ 1,155,261.55
45	69	$ -	$ 1,220,501.00	$ 62,789.00	$ 60,000.00	$ 1,160,501.00	$ 86,000.00	$ -	$ 1,127,024.63
46	70	$ -	$ 1,285,937.00	$ 65,436.00	$ 60,000.00	$ 1,225,937.00	$ 86,000.00	$ -	$ 1,097,375.86
47	71	$ -	$ 1,354,026.00	$ 68,089.00	$ 60,000.00	$ 1,294,026.00	$ 86,000.00	$ -	$ 1,066,244.66
48	72	$ -	$ 1,424,807.00	$ 70,781.00	$ 60,000.00	$ 1,364,807.00	$ 86,000.00	$ -	$ 1,033,556.89
49	73	$ -	$ 1,498,214.00	$ 73,407.00	$ 60,000.00	$ 1,438,214.00	$ 86,000.00	$ -	$ 999,234.73
50	74	$ -	$ 1,574,270.00	$ 76,056.00	$ 60,000.00	$ 1,514,270.00	$ 86,000.00	$ -	$ 963,196.47
51	75	$ -	$ 1,652,947.00	$ 78,677.00	$ 60,000.00	$ 1,592,947.00	$ 86,000.00	$ -	$ 925,356.29
52	76	$ -	$ 1,734,183.00	$ 81,236.00	$ 60,000.00	$ 1,674,183.00	$ 86,000.00	$ -	$ 885,624.11
53	77	$ -	$ 1,817,948.00	$ 83,766.00	$ 60,000.00	$ 1,757,948.00	$ 86,000.00	$ -	$ 843,905.31
54	78	$ -	$ 1,904,182.00	$ 86,234.00	$ 60,000.00	$ 1,944,182.00	$ 86,000.00	$ -	$ 800,100.58
55	79	$ -	$ 1,992,953.00	$ 88,771.00	$ 60,000.00	$ 1,932,953.00	$ 86,000.00	$ -	$ 754,105.61
56	80	$ -	$ 2,084,324.00	$ 91,371.00	$ 60,000.00	$ 2,024,324.00	$ 86,000.00	$ -	$ 705,810.89
57	81	$ -	$ 2,178,435.00	$ 94,111.00	$ 60,000.00	$ 2,118,435.00	$ 86,000.00	$ -	$ 655,101.43
58	82	$ -	$ 2,275,456.00	$ 97,021.00	$ 60,000.00	$ 2,215,456.00	$ 86,000.00	$ -	$ 601,856.51
59	83	$ -	$ 2,375,616.00	$ 100,160.00	$ 60,000.00	$ 2,315,616.00	$ 86,000.00	$ -	$ 545,949.33
60	84	$ -	$ 2,479,094.00	$ 103,478.00	$ 60,000.00	$ 2,419,094.00	$ 86,000.00	$ -	$ 487,246.80
61	85	$ -	$ 2,584,917.00	$ 105,823.00	$ 60,000.00	$ 2,524,917.00	$ 86,000.00	$ -	$ 425,609.14
62	86	$ -	$ 2,694,075.00	$ 109,158.00	$ 60,000.00	$ 2,634,075.00	$ 86,000.00	$ -	$ 360,989.59
63	87	$ -	$ 2,806,256.00	$ 112,181.00	$ 60,000.00	$ 2,746,256.00	$ 86,000.00	$ -	$ 292,934.07
64	88	$ -	$ 2,921,092.00	$ 114,836.00	$ 60,000.00	$ 2,861,092.00	$ 86,000.00	$ -	$ 221,580.78
65	89	$ -	$ 3,038,008.00	$ 116,916.00	$ 60,000.00	$ 2,978,008.00	$ 86,000.00	$ -	$ 146,659.82
66	90	$ -	$ 3,156,473.00	$ 118,465.00	$ 60,000.00	$ 3,096,473.00	$ 86,000.00	$ -	$ 67,992.81
									-$ 14,607.55

NOTES:		Life Insurance	5.0% Compounded Annually
	1	Numbers above are samples from a real policy.	Numbers are based on annual compound with no loss.
	2	You save $11,545 each year from age 28 to age 47 and put it towards the premiums in a life insurance.	You save up at age 25 and start your investment account at the end of age 25. No interest has accumulated yet.
	3	Total saved over 20 years (age 28 to 47) = $230,900. By age 32, the growth of the cash value is more than premiums. By age 38, the cash value surpasses the annual premium. By age 43, the cash value equals the total premium that will be put into the policy.	Total saved over 40 years (age 25 to 64) = $408,000.
	4	Retire at age 65 and begin to borrow from your life insurance. The growth of the cash value is $52,682 and increasing each year.	Retire at age 65 and start withdrawing to receive $60,000 after taxes ($86,000 required assuming 30% of gross income goes towards tax).
	5	Retirement amount available at age 65 = $984,831.	Retirement amount available at age 65 = $1,207,765.
	6	By age 90 there will be more than enough to continue.	By age 90, there will be no money left.

Fig. 3-2. Whole Life VS. 5%

Although PDPWLI is the method we have implemented in our lives, within it are many options available that only a professional can help you with in selecting what is the best fit for you. Everyone's situation is different and a true professional would ask questions to ensure the right fit for you and your family. They will also make sure you understand what it is you are getting into so that you have control of your hard earned money. What we have shown here is just utilizing insurance for the comfort of possible retirement. This only scratches the surface of what you can do with insurance especially when you apply the Infinite Banking Concept to it! You can finance the items in your life, utilize it for investments and much more! We believe that this concept truly is the foundation of how one is able to Make More and Work Less.

For more information about how this concept works, we highly recommend the books, *Becoming your Own Banker - Unlocking the Infinite Banking Concept* by R. Nelson Nash and *The Banker's Secret* by Glen Zacher and Jayson Lowe of McGuire Financial. We had the honor of meeting Mr. Nash and can say absolutely that his book has transformed our lives. We would also like to thank Richard Canfield, our Infinite Banker Expert and Insurance Broker for introducing this concept to us. It has literally changed our lives. Feel free to contact us for more information.

Don't be boxed in with what everyone else says, do your own research and come to your own conclusions.

Chapter - 4 -

Find Land, Make More

After talking about insurance our first and most important pillar to Make More and Work Less, we step up the risk factor a little and construct our second pillar of financial foundation: Land.

Why Land?

From the beginning of time, land has been a symbol of wealth and power. Land is taken over when wars are won. Power is determined according to the amount of land one has. Land is a commodity that can never be created and can only be consumed. Because of that, land, over a period of time will always hold value, if not become more valuable. If time is on your side, land will always be a good place to park your money.

There are many ways to invest in land. Two of the most common methods are: Buy, Hold and Sell; or Buy and Build.

Buying Raw Land

The general idea here is to purchase raw land, be it large or small and wait until the closest town or business comes and wants to buy your land. Raw land is generally undeveloped farm land that is away from large cities and towns. Due to the fact that it is undeveloped and away from the amenities of the city, raw land is generally cheap to purchase. However sufficient research must be done and time must be on your side. The last thing you want to do is purchase a large area of land that nobody wants.

When purchasing raw land, there are four things you must consider: population growth, the increase of jobs, accessibility to major roads and services and demographics of the nearby city. If you find land on the outskirts of a large city that has an upward trend in population, you can generally predict that the city will thrive and grow for a period of time. Some examples of upward trend in population include: internal growth or immigration from other cities, a steady creation of jobs and need for more workers, has relatively easy access to large bodies of water and highways and has a relatively large group of people in the prime years of their lives and younger. When the time comes where the city reaches the land that you own for it to expand, the city will need to buy your land back. Since land value has increased, you will reap the benefits of purchasing that land from years ago. However, this strategy is a long-term strategy that can take anywhere from 4 to 5 years to as much as 10 to 15 years. Land also is something that is generally bought with cash unless you have a structured plan and the right systems in place to get funding from banking institutions.

Another situation that may arise is if your land is within close vicinity to commodities, such as oil, minerals, water and natural resources. Mining companies and oil companies may need the land to build infrastructure for mining or processing the natural resources. At this time, you will also benefit from the raw land that you have purchased years ago. Again for raw land to be an effective strategy for you, you must have long-term goals and sufficient knowledge of the land you are purchasing.

Build Up or Divide

Buying land in developed areas also can be a great strategy. Vacant or empty lots in developed, sought after neighborhoods can be a great opportunity. Like raw land, one must have great knowledge of the neighborhood before making such a decision. Questions such as: What can we build? A single family home? A duplex? A 6-plex? An apartment complex? A condo? An office building? What would this property be worth after it is built? What is the going rents or leases here? What are the vacancies here? How much will building cost me? How will I fund the construction and the materials? How long will it take to build? How much time do I have until I need the property to be sold, rented or leased?

All these questions and more must be answered before you make the decision to purchase the lot. The same can be assessed with run down, old and vacant properties. Account for the demolition costs, permits or zoning cost and time as well.

This strategy can be very profitable. For example let's say you purchased an old property for $185,000 and the lot allows for a 4-plex to be built and you know that the 4-plex can be sold for $950,000 when all is completed. If it costs $600,000 to build the 4-plex, say another $60,000 for all the permits, paper work, accounting, lawyer fees and holding costs. One can profit $100,000 in approximately a year, accounting for building time and selling time. If you have the right people in place and the right numbers assessed, you can possibly not be too involved in the process and reap the benefits of the profits because you have the foresight of the land's potential.

Another method of utilizing existing land is to purchase the land and then subdivide the area so that you can sell each divided area or develop each area separately. For example, say you bought a piece of land that currently has a small house on it. Based on your research you can divide this land into four smaller narrower lots. You can sell two of the lots and use the money from the profits to build two properties on your remaining lots and basically have all your money back. Or you can build four properties on the four lots, get a mortgage on all four properties and rent them out. By mortgaging the properties, you have recovered all the money that you have put into the land and building of the properties, have money to do something else, plus now you have four investment properties! Real Estate gurus like Donald Trump uses this strategy to build the empires that they have now. Again, a lot of research must be done about the area to be sufficient. Keep in mind that buying very run down properties and land will generally require cash as most banking institutions will not lend on land. However, if done correctly this strategy can be very profitable.

I Have Little Money, How Can I Get Into Land?

Most people understand that land is a valuable asset and would love to have land in their portfolios, however most people generally do not have the funds needed to buy land out right or fund the materials and labor for developing and building a property. A concept called Land Banking can help you invest in land for a fraction of the cost.

Land Banking is similar to the buying raw land concept, with one twist – multiple sources of funds. There are companies out there that look for investors with $100,000, $60,000, $10,000 even as little as $5,000 that they want to invest. These companies combine money from many investors and they use the money to buy raw land. They do all the research and all the assessments before buying the land. They zone the land and at times partly develop the land so that when the city needs to expand into that area, they will need to pay a premium for the land. Once this happens all the investors will get their shares of the profits of the sale. These companies do all research, paperwork and selling of the land.

Generally speaking these companies can potentially double your investment every five to seven years! If that is the case and if you are in your 30s, you have about five to six cycles of five to seven years before you retire. Therefore, if you were to invest $10,000 in land banking today and keep reinvesting the principle and profits back into land banking, then by the time you are at your retirement age of 65, your $10,000 will be $640,000. Looking back to our numbers in Chapter 2, the ideal retirement number is $1.5 million. That means that, if you invested $25,000 one time at age 30, you will have achieved that goal, whereas people at the banks require $25,000 each year. Talk about Making More and Working Less.

There are many different types of investments that are similar to that of Land Banking. Ones that provide you with great returns, but may be a little riskier than what people are use to. In the case of Land Banking, you will need to account for time as the risk factor. If you are placing money away in your retirement plans and will not be accessing them anyway, why not diversify some of those funds into Land Banking or other exempt market products. And yes, exempt market products are generally eligible for government supported retirement tax deferral programs. Therefore, a good strategy is to invest some into exempt markets, get the tax benefit and instead of using the tax benefit on everyday items, reinvest the tax return into more exempt market products for the following year, basically allowing it to self-fund itself.

Explore the Possibilities

Take the time and expose yourselves to Land Banking and other exempt market products and companies. You will be surprised how many different opportunities there are that may not be as risky as you once thought after you understand the concepts and structures. For more information, please contact us and we can get you connected to the experts in this arena. To download a copy of the following chart, for easier viewing, see www.makemoreworklessbook.com.

Set your goals high and explore your opportunities.

Let's compare saving with Land Banking VS What most are doing as mentioned in Chapter 2.

Land Banking versus 5.0% Compounded Annually

Year	Age	Deposit (for Land Banking case)	Account Amount (for Land Banking case)	Growth in Account (for Land Banking case)	Withdrawal (for Land Banking case)	Account Amount after Withdrawal (for Land Banking case)	Withdrawal (from 5.0% investment account)	Deposit at end of year (for 5.0% case)	Account Amount at end of year (for 5.0% case)
1	25	$10,000.00	$10,000.00	$ -	$ -	$ -	$ -	$10,200.00	$10,200.00
2	26	$10,000.00	$20,000.00	$ -	$ -	$ -	$ -	$10,200.00	$20,910.00
3	27	$10,000.00	$30,000.00	$ -	$ -	$ -	$ -	$10,200.00	$32,155.50
4	28	$10,000.00	$40,000.00	$ -	$ -	$ -	$ -	$10,200.00	$43,963.28
5	29	$ -	$40,000.00	$ -	$ -	$ -	$ -	$10,200.00	$56,361.44
6	30	$ -	$40,000.00	$ -	$ -	$ -	$ -	$10,200.00	$69,379.51
7	31	$ -	$40,000.00	$10,000.00	$ -	$ -	$ -	$10,200.00	$83,048.49
8	32	$ -	$50,000.00	$10,000.00	$ -	$ -	$ -	$10,200.00	$97,400.91
9	33	$ -	$60,000.00	$10,000.00	$ -	$ -	$ -	$10,200.00	$112,470.96
10	34	$ -	$70,000.00	$10,000.00	$ -	$ -	$ -	$10,200.00	$128,294.50
11	35	$ -	$70,000.00	$ -	$ -	$ -	$ -	$10,200.00	$144,909.23
12	36	$ -	$70,000.00	$ -	$ -	$ -	$ -	$10,200.00	$162,354.69
13	37	$ -	$90,000.00	$20,000.00	$ -	$ -	$ -	$10,200.00	$180,672.43
14	38	$ -	$110,000.00	$20,000.00	$ -	$ -	$ -	$10,200.00	$199,906.05
15	39	$ -	$130,000.00	$20,000.00	$ -	$ -	$ -	$10,200.00	$220,101.35
16	40	$ -	$150,000.00	$20,000.00	$ -	$ -	$ -	$10,200.00	$241,306.42
17	41	$ -	$150,000.00	$ -	$ -	$ -	$ -	$10,200.00	$263,571.74
18	42	$ -	$150,000.00	$ -	$ -	$ -	$ -	$10,200.00	$286,950.32
19	43	$ -	$190,000.00	$40,000.00	$ -	$ -	$ -	$10,200.00	$311,497.84
20	44	$ -	$230,000.00	$40,000.00	$ -	$ -	$ -	$10,200.00	$337,272.73
21	45	$ -	$270,000.00	$40,000.00	$ -	$ -	$ -	$10,200.00	$364,336.37
22	46	$ -	$310,000.00	$40,000.00	$ -	$ -	$ -	$10,200.00	$392,753.19
23	47	$ -	$310,000.00	$ -	$ -	$ -	$ -	$10,200.00	$422,590.85
24	48	$ -	$310,000.00	$ -	$ -	$ -	$ -	$10,200.00	$453,920.39
25	49	$ -	$390,000.00	$80,000.00	$ -	$ -	$ -	$10,200.00	$486,816.41
26	50	$ -	$470,000.00	$80,000.00	$ -	$ -	$ -	$10,200.00	$521,357.23
27	51	$ -	$550,000.00	$80,000.00	$ -	$ -	$ -	$10,200.00	$557,625.09
28	52	$ -	$630,000.00	$80,000.00	$ -	$ -	$ -	$10,200.00	$595,706.34
29	53	$ -	$630,000.00	$ -	$ -	$ -	$ -	$10,200.00	$635,691.66
30	54	$ -	$630,000.00	$ -	$ -	$ -	$ -	$10,200.00	$677,676.24
31	55	$ -	$790,000.00	$160,000.00	$ -	$ -	$ -	$10,200.00	$721,760.06
32	56	$ -	$950,000.00	$160,000.00	$ -	$ -	$ -	$10,200.00	$768,048.06
33	57	$ -	$1,110,000.00	$160,000.00	$ -	$ -	$ -	$10,200.00	$816,650.46
34	58	$ -	$1,270,000.00	$160,000.00	$ -	$ -	$ -	$10,200.00	$867,682.99
35	59	$ -	$1,270,000.00	$ -	$ -	$ -	$ -	$10,200.00	$921,267.13
36	60	$ -	$1,270,000.00	$ -	$ -	$ -	$ -	$10,200.00	$977,530.49
37	61	$ -	$1,590,000.00	$320,000.00	$ -	$ -	$ -	$10,200.00	$1,036,607.02
38	62	$ -	$1,910,000.00	$320,000.00	$ -	$ -	$ -	$10,200.00	$1,098,637.37
39	63	$ -	$2,230,000.00	$320,000.00	$ -	$ -	$ -	$10,200.00	$1,163,769.24
40	64	$ -	$2,550,000.00	$320,000.00	$ -	$ -	$ -	$10,200.00	$1,232,157.70
41	65	$ -	$2,550,000.00	$ -	$ -	$ -	$86,000.00	$ -	$1,207,765.58
42	66	$ -	$2,550,000.00	$ -	$86,000.00	$2,464,000.00	$86,000.00	$ -	$1,182,153.86
43	67	$ -	$2,464,000.00	$ -	$86,000.00	$2,378,000.00	$86,000.00	$ -	$1,155,261.55
44	68	$ -	$2,378,000.00	$ -	$86,000.00	$2,292,000.00	$86,000.00	$ -	$1,127,024.63
45	69	$ -	$2,292,000.00	$ -	$86,000.00	$2,206,000.00	$86,000.00	$ -	$1,097,375.86
46	70	$ -	$2,206,000.00	$ -	$86,000.00	$2,034,000.00	$86,000.00	$ -	$1,066,244.66
47	71	$ -	$2,120,000.00	$ -	$86,000.00	$2,034,000.00	$86,000.00	$ -	$1,033,556.89
48	72	$ -	$2,034,000.00	$ -	$86,000.00	$1,948,000.00	$86,000.00	$ -	$999,234.73
49	73	$ -	$1,948,000.00	$ -	$86,000.00	$1,862,000.00	$86,000.00	$ -	$963,196.47
50	74	$ -	$1,862,000.00	$ -	$86,000.00	$1,776,000.00	$86,000.00	$ -	$925,356.29
51	75	$ -	$1,776,000.00	$ -	$86,000.00	$1,690,000.00	$86,000.00	$ -	$885,624.11
52	76	$ -	$1,690,000.00	$ -	$86,000.00	$1,604,000.00	$86,000.00	$ -	$843,905.31
53	77	$ -	$1,604,000.00	$ -	$86,000.00	$1,518,000.00	$86,000.00	$ -	$800,100.58
54	78	$ -	$1,518,000.00	$ -	$86,000.00	$1,432,000.00	$86,000.00	$ -	$754,105.61
55	79	$ -	$1,432,000.00	$ -	$86,000.00	$1,346,000.00	$86,000.00	$ -	$705,810.89
56	80	$ -	$1,346,000.00	$ -	$86,000.00	$1,260,000.00	$86,000.00	$ -	$655,101.43
57	81	$ -	$1,260,000.00	$ -	$86,000.00	$1,174,000.00	$86,000.00	$ -	$601,856.51
58	82	$ -	$1,174,000.00	$ -	$86,000.00	$1,088,000.00	$86,000.00	$ -	$546,949.33
59	83	$ -	$1,088,000.00	$ -	$86,000.00	$1,002,000.00	$86,000.00	$ -	$487,246.80
60	84	$ -	$1,002,000.00	$ -	$86,000.00	$916,000.00	$86,000.00	$ -	$425,609.14
61	85	$ -	$916,000.00	$ -	$86,000.00	$830,000.00	$86,000.00	$ -	$360,889.59
62	86	$ -	$830,000.00	$ -	$86,000.00	$744,000.00	$86,000.00	$ -	$292,934.07
63	87	$ -	$744,000.00	$ -	$86,000.00	$658,000.00	$86,000.00	$ -	$221,580.78
64	88	$ -	$658,000.00	$ -	$86,000.00	$572,000.00	$86,000.00	$ -	$146,659.82
65	89	$ -	$572,000.00	$ -	$86,000.00	$486,000.00	$86,000.00	$ -	$87,992.81
66	90	$ -	$486,000.00	$ -	$86,000.00	$400,000.00	$86,000.00	$ -	-$14,607.55

NOTES:

	Land Banking	5.0% Compounded Annually
1	Numbers above are based on an assumption of doubling every 6 years.	Numbers are based on annual compound with no loss.
2	You save $10,000 each year from age 25 to age 28 and put it towards land banking.	You save up at age 25 and start your investment account at the end of age 25. No interest has accumulated yet.
3	Total saved over 4 years (age 25 to 28) = $40,000.	Total saved over 40 years (age 25 to 64) = $408,000.
4	Retire at age 65 and start withdrawing to receive $60,000 after taxes ($86,000 required assuming 30% of gross income goes towards taxes). This is assuming that the land banking investment was done through RRSP and you are no longer reinvesting, which means that you will no longer double your growth.	Retire at age 65 and start withdrawing to receive $60,000 after taxes ($86,000 required assuming 30% of gross income goes towards tax).
5	Retirement amount available at age 65 = $2,550,000	Retirement amount available at age 65 = $1,207,765.
6	By age 90 there will be enough to continue for another few years.	By age 90, there will be no money left.

Fig. 4-1. Land Banking VS. 5%

Chapter - 5 -

Have Metals, Make More

Now that two of the four pillars of financial foundation have been established, we can introduce another pillar. The concept is well-known and is as old as insurance and land if not older. Our third pillar is none other than the tried-and-true gold, silver and other commodities.

History Lesson

Throughout time, commodities, such as gold and silver have always held their value. They always have and always will be a great place to park your hard earned money. As long as governments continue to devalue currency, gold and silver will always have a place in everyone's portfolio. So why aren't more people holding onto gold and silver? Well, many people do not understand why our society is the way it is. Why do we have these recent mortgage crises, credit crises and economic busts? Well, it all has to do with the fact that gold is no longer connected to the value of currency, which is all about credit. There isn't anything keeping the value of currency stable.

Before 1970, U.S. banks were required to have a set amount of gold in their vaults to support the amount of money they had in their bank. Therefore, if anything happened and people who had money in the bank wanted their money back, the bank would have had enough gold to secure them. However, during 1971, the gold convertibility was severed from currency. Banks started lending money without any actual backing. In a sense, banks are literally creating money from thin air. They are saturating the economy and reducing the value of what the dollar can buy. Proof of this happened instantly. In 1972, we needed $35 to buy one ounce of gold. When gold was removed from the currency, gold required $38 and $42 in 1973. It now sells at

$1,300 for an ounce at the time of writing this book. We illustrate the American banking system here because it is a universally known case. For Canadians, the fiat system started in 1933.

This creating of money or fractionalizing sadly is what happened throughout history. To understand what is happening in our society, we can simply look back to ancient Rome. The Roman Empire was continually expanding and growing, taking in new lands and bringing in more and more people. As the reaches of Rome got farther and farther, the cost of getting food and supplies to those areas got more and more expensive. During this time, the currency being used was gold, silver or copper coins for the trading of goods and services. To account for all the additional costs for food and travel, the Roman Empire decided to debase the currency. They began to mix the precious metals with cheaper metals so that there was more money. It also was cheaper to make. So on the outside, the two coins looked the same, but in reality, one has less gold content than the other. Furthermore, they took these debased coins and they started to scrape off the edges of "actual" gold and used the combination of many gold scrapings, melted it down, to create even more coins. There were more coins in the marketplace but the value of the coins was getting diluted.

Say you were to buy some bread that normally cost one gold coin. You hand the merchant one gold coin. The merchant would compare your gold coin with his pure gold coin and say, "Hmmm your gold coin is a little different. It's a little smaller and a little lighter. If you want the bread, you will need to give me two of these gold coins that you have." The value of the bread did not change; neither did the size of the bread. But because of the diluted value of the gold coin, the cost of bread increased.

Today

This is exactly what is happening in our society right now. Cost of living is going up year after year and more and more money is being pumped into the market place to bail out companies and national debts. Before banks were limited by the amount of gold they had in their system as to how much they could lend. Today, banks only need to keep a fraction of the funds deposited with them on hand. That is, banks can lend $10 for every $1 that is in their system! In some countries, that ratio is infinite! It is free reign to print money.

So What Does This Have to Do With Gold and Silver?

In less than 50 years, the cost of gold has gone from $35 in 1972 to $1,300 in 2013! Although gold and silver can be volatile commodities, the trend of both metals have been upwards. This is because the governments will always continue to create money and devalue the currency. It happened in Rome; it happened in Germany during the Great Depression in 1929; it happened in Japan, which led to its economic crisis; and it is happening today in the United States and Canada. Gold and silver will always retain its value because it is the purest form of currency.

OK I Understand Why Gold Is Important, But Why Silver?

Silver is like the little brother of gold. It follows the trends of what happens with its big brother. Historically speaking, silver should have a ratio of 12 to 16 to 1 with gold. Meaning every ounce of gold, is worth 12 to 16 ounces of silver. However, due the lack of inflation adjustment and other economic and industrial reasons, that ratio is 65 to 1! This means the potential of silver is a lot higher. There are also a lot more industrial uses for silver, such as cell phones, medicine and electronics. Silver also is considered the poor man's gold because it is so much more affordable in comparison. If people wanted to start investing in commodities and they only had a few hundred dollars, they can purchase 25 to 30 one-ounce silver coins instead of half an ounce of gold. It gives them more flexibility and is easier to distribute if need be.

Story Time

The point here is to get people aware of what other options there are besides the traditional sense of savings and investing. If you want to start small, then start small. If you want to put more into it, then go ahead. Do what you feel you can handle comfortably. For ourselves, a simple story got us excited to do something and invest in gold and silver.

It was about a group of lower income individuals that banded together and bought one silver coin a week. Even though they were all struggling to put food on the table they were all committed to contribute enough together to get one silver coin a week. Their collection grew and grew over time as did the value of silver. Soon, with the amount of silver they collected and the value of silver, they had enough to sell it all and get a vending machine. With the vending machine, they now had cash coming. They got another machine and another. We were so inspired and looked at it from our perspective. If people struggling to put food on the table, can get one silver coin a week, then we must be able to get something! The important thing here is consistency and discipline. If you said that you will do something, then do it. Whether it is buying one gold ounce a month, 10 gold ounces a month or one silver coin a month, you will be surprised what difference it will make over a period of time.

Strategy?

If you are indeed interested in investing in commodities like gold and silver, two great sources are www.goldandsilver.com and www.kitco.com. When buying commodities, whether in large quantities or small amounts depending on your strategy, it will require different amounts of research and education. If you are looking to buy and sell quickly, then gold and silver stocks and paper is the way to go. However, keep in mind that there are a lot more stocks and paper than the actual gold or silver. This means that if everyone wanted to exchange their stocks or paper for their gold or silver, not everyone will get their share. Control over these investments is also very limited.

Personally, we like to purchase minted one-ounce gold and silver coins. You pay a little more for the government minting but you know that it is legitimate. In Canada, both gold and silver are minted with 99.99 percent pure gold or silver, and in the United States, they are minted with 99.9 percent purity. The extra 0.09 percent purity will not make a difference in resale or purchase price but is something that is good to know when buying these coins. Another advantage of purchasing actual coinage is the fact that you get to have it in your hand, it is yours and you can secure it however you like. We recommend storing your metals in private storage facilities rather than security boxes at banks where once again your access and control is limited. Due to the size of coinage, chances of counterfeiting, plating or drilling out metal is very low, another reason why coinage has its positives. Having coinage will be easier for resale as well, because it is easy to prove authenticity and opens up a larger market place versus selling 100 ounce bars where your customer base is a lot smaller.

American Gold - 1 ounce eagle

American Silver - 1 ounce eagle

Canadian Gold - 1 ounce maple

Canadian Silver - 1 ounce maple

My Bank Sells Gold and Silver Is That Where I Can Get Them?

Some banks sell gold and silver, but very few branches actually have them there to give you after you purchase them. Many of them will take your order, and you will need to wait a few days for your coins to come. Banks generally add on service, administration and shipping charges as well to each coin. Our recommendation is to go search online for coin shops and precious metal dealers around your area. You can ask around what their prices are. Like any business, coin shops will compete for your business so prices vary from shop to shop. We recommend finding vendors who can build a relationship with you and go to them consistently. Vendors will usually give preferred prices to you if you are a repeating customer and you will see that they will charge far less than your bank does.

I Have Gold and Silver Where Can I Sell It?

When gold and silver have made their jumps in the market place or you have held them long enough and are happy with the potential returns, there are many options as to where you can sell. Online options are very popular. Other investors within your circle and even selling back to your vendors could be profitable options.

By diversifying into hard asset commodities, not only are you preserving the value of your money, but you may also benefit greatly from the continuous money printing that is going on in our society. Combined with insurance and land banking, you surely will Make More and Work Less.

**Don't just rely on one strategy, diversify
and hedge your opportunities.**

Chapter - 6 -

Share More, Make More

Before we get to our final pillar, we want to talk a little about two items that play a great factor in your success. It enables the previous three pillars of financial foundation to grow. We are talking about: Networking and Building Relationships.

The most common questions with networking are where and how? Focus on relationships. People do business and invest with people they like and trust. Why do you buy certain items knowing that something out there is better? You did so because you felt a bond or relationship with the salesperson. We no longer need to sell to people. Everyone is ready to buy. They already have educated themselves about certain products before they go looking for it. With the information on the Internet, we are able to compare, check prices and read reviews. What they don't expect is someone who is there to add value to their purchase or to enhance their buying experience. It is those salespeople who customers will go back to and request their services. Why? It is the relationship that has been built one transaction at a time.

Three keys to successful networking are:

- Key No. 1 - LISTEN more than talk
- Key No. 2 - Explain How VALUE can be added
- Key No. 3 - NEVER sell

LISTEN more than talk

Have you ever noticed that when you are with people who like to talk, and after an evening with them, they say that they enjoyed the evening a lot and that it was great talking to you even if they did all the talking? Humans by nature like the sound of their own voice. When you genuinely express interest in what someone has to say, you would be surprised how much they want to tell you. This is why we were given two ears and one mouth. So that we listen twice as much as we speak. By nature, we are fearful of silence. If no one is talking, everyone will develop an urge to want to say something and get a conversation going again. Topics, such as families, hobbies, vacation and work are usually great conversation starters. Not only do you get to learn more about certain topics that you may have never thought of, but you will also learn a lot more about the person you are talking to and while doing so, build a relationship. Having an engineering background, most of the people around us talk about construction, oil and gas and steel. Never in our right mind would we have thought we'd meet a crime scene clean up expert, a professional mixed martial arts fighter or a former Snow White at Disneyland! The stories that they shared and what we have learned about their occupations further allowed us to have a wider range of topics for us to talk about and stories to share. Before long, you will find that you will have something to add with any topic as you will be able to connect different industries and stories that you've heard before with new people that you are meeting.

How VALUE can be Added

As you are listening to what the other person is saying, you must also keep something very important in mind. The Golden Key to building relationships is: "How can I add value to this person?" People today are so busy thinking about themselves that it is very rare that someone would have their best interest in mind. Not only are you listening intently to what they are saying, but also have their best interest in mind. If you have this question in mind, you will start to look for areas where you can add value to what they are saying. Whether it's someone you can introduce them to, who will solve their problem, or if it is something that you have that can assist them, or information that you know that can save them time. Looking for opportunities to add value will be a great step in building a relationship. Our minds are set to reciprocate what we receive. If you were to add value to someone, chances are great that, the favor will be returned and usually, in much greater ways than you would have thought. If you were going into a conversation with people who you know could help you with something, it is always better for them to suggest their assistance than to have you ask for it. But how can this happen? By adding value. What can you do to make things easier for them? What can you provide that would make them feel special? The return may not come immediately or at times at all, but when it does, you can be assured that a great relationship may be in the making.

Recently, our real estate agent has offered to list a few of our properties and sell them for no fee! This was a complete surprise to us. Never would we have thought that we could get a deal like that. Getting a couple of percentage points off, we could see, but for free? We were taken aback. Even so, we have agreed to offer him a fee for his services as we also value his time and effort. The point is before he offered, we never asked about a discount or special rates. What we have been doing is, connecting him to our network of investors and team members, shared information and materials. Once you realize that there are a lot more things that one can offer besides money, you'll be able to see more creative ways to add value to others.

Another example of adding value is how we treat our tenants, to be discussed later on in this book. By putting ourselves in the shoes of our tenants, we were able to think of ways to add value to their moving-in experience, which, in turn, led them to sending us referrals. Due to all the value we provided our tenants, they wanted their friends and family to have the same treatment and therefore, recommended us to help them.

NEVER sell

Networking key No. 3 is never sell to the person you are talking to. The last thing you want to do is to have a potential client or partner label you as a "used car salesman." We all have this person in mind: someone who is only pushing for the sale, hiding the truth on certain items, not genuine, constantly talking about how great they are and why you need to buy. If those are the people that you stay away from, then those are the people that you definitely do not want to become. The fact is, as long as you follow the first two keys: listen intently and look to add value, you will automatically not sell. You will find that you will answer questions and add information about what you do know when prompted and only because the person you are talking to genuinely wanted to hear more about what you have to say.

Always remember to read your audience. Look at their body language. Are they checking their watch? Are they eyeing the door? Are they leaning forward? Are they responding to your information positively?

Listen to their responses. Are they replying with skepticism or with excitement? Are they yawning or speaking very slowly? These are clues as to whether the information you are telling them is adding value or not. As long as you pay attention to your listener, you will find that avoiding the dreaded "used car salesman" stereotype is very natural.

Relationships Built

When we were being approached with insurance, land banking, and gold and silver deals, we weren't being sold. They showed what value they can provide us. In turn, great relationships have been built because of that. A bond is formed where we want to add value back to them and in doing so, they add value to us furthermore. Each party feels the need and wants to talk and promote the other parties' skills, services and/or products. Having other people talk about you is much more effective than you talking about yourself.

Other Avenues of Income

One industry that thrives on this principle is network marketing. We know, network marketing is an industry that has gotten a really bad reputation. Instantly, people relate it to a Ponzi or pyramid scheme. They close their minds and do not give themselves a chance to hear what it is they could be missing. The fact is that we do this every day. Network Marketing is nothing more than recommending and promoting something you use and like.

Be open to the products and how the system works. Network marketing companies, can be successful companies who base their success on sharing what they love and use personally with their family and friends, who in turn, share with their family and friends and so on. You are doing that anyway when you recommend a friend to a restaurant or a movie, why not recommend a product that you personally use and get paid for it? Before you know it, you may have another stream of revenue coming. Most importantly, if you decided on something, follow up and follow through on it, by doing so, you will Make More and Work Less.

**The more information you share,
the more people you help.**

**The more people you help,
the more you will get in return.**

Chapter - 7 -

Hold Paper, Make More

A structure with two legs will not be stable in one direction, now that you have constructed three pillars, your plan to Make More and Work Less can stand on its own. With insurance, land banking and precious metals already in your portfolio along with other sources of income, such as other exempt market products and network marketing you can probably already see how you can:

1) Reduce your time to work for retirement.
2) Have an even more comfortable life before and after retirement.
3) See an opportunity to do what you want on your own terms.

What if we were to say that we can add another piece to your structure and make all those possibilities happen even faster and provide you a life you only dreamed of?

The Fourth Pillar of Financial Foundation

The final pillar is Real Estate. Over time, real estate has proved to be one of the best vehicles of where to place your money. It is a process. Some people think real estate is risky and too much hard work, however, there are ways to make it less risky, easier and enjoyable. All business gurus out there and financial experts have real estate in their portfolio in one shape or form. Regardless of where their funds were accumulated, be it from stocks, from selling businesses, from their insurance, from their precious metals, eventually it will get converted into real estate in some way. People will always need a place to stay and the population is always growing. Regardless of how poor a market is or how great a market is, real estate will always hold value over time (similar to land). Demand for real estate is so varied that as long as you manage your risk, there will always be a market for what you are offering.

For one to be successful in real estate, three keys that we have discussed before are even more important than anything else: Mindset, Networking and Building Relationships. All those real estate experts that tell you that you can make quick and easy money in real estate are not telling you exactly what to expect. It is true that you CAN make money quickly and easily, but that is only after you have put in the work. Everything gets easier over time, but it will take the proper mindset, networking and relationship building to get you there.

Main Forms of Real Estate Opportunities

Another very important key to real estate is knowing what exit strategy to use before you enter an investment opportunity. Our goal is to Make More and Work Less and therefore, proper planning and risk assessment is very important. There are many types of properties, such as single family homes, duplexes, condos, multi-family, etc. and likewise, many different exit strategies.

The four main investing exit strategies are:

1. Wholesale - Short-Term Capital without owning
2. Rent to Own - Short/Long-Term Cashflow
3. Buy-Fix-Flip - Short-Term Capital Generator
4. Buy-Hold - Long-Term Cashflow Opportunity

Wholesaling

Wholesaling properties is a method where you as the

investor will never hold the property, but only the contract. You then find a buyer for that property who you will then double close with for a fee.

For example, let's say you have agreed to terms with Jill to buy her property for $200,000, down from the initial asking price of $220,000 and have signed the contract. You now have about 10 business days to secure a buyer for that property. From your list of buyers that are interested in this type of property which you have developed through networking, you found Paul who would like to buy the property. You and Paul then agree that he will buy the property from you for $205,000. At the date of possession of the house from Jill to you, you will close the deal with Jill, and hours later, after you get the keys, close your deal with Paul. At the end of the day, you have made $5,000 without ever taking possession of the property.

Wholesaling

Contract to sell to you   Contract to sell to Paul

Hold the Contract

JILL → YOU → PAUL

$200,000 $5000 $205,000
                  Profit

Wholesaling is one of the easiest ways of creating capital with minimal capital. As you can see in the example, you will never need to take possession of the property meaning you will never need the full capital to purchase the property. You are getting paid for selling the contract to someone else who wants the property that you have secured on paper. If you were unable to find a buyer in time, you can always renegotiate with the seller for a longer condition time or let the property go and work on another property. The risk to you is minimal.

Keys to Wholesaling

To do wholesaling successfully, you must have a good system in place. Finding motivated sellers willing to sell their property below market value, being able to assess appropriately the potential value of the property and finding the buyer for the property are the main factors.

Finding Motivated Sellers

Why would anyone want to sell at below market value? People's situations are different. They may be in great need to sell because of a loss in the family, a job change, job loss, a divorce or the property is too run down for them to maintain it. The fact is that you never know unless you ask or look for the opportunities. In many cases, people are willing to sell at below market value so they can avoid going into foreclosure or to get rid of the headache of maintaining it. Advertising, going door to door, handing out flyers, looking at newspapers and checking for garage sales are all potential ways you can find motivated sellers.

Assessing the Property Value

To know if you have a property under market value, you'll need to have an agent help you with numbers. Find great real estate agents who will work with you and get you comparables of other properties in the area. In the example above, if the property is in good living condition and the comparables in the area show that the property is worth $225,000, then you have gotten the property at a great deal for $200,000. You then pass the great deal to Paul for $5,000 who can move in right away, without having to negotiate a deal with the seller himself.

Another likely scenario is that Jill's property is really in bad shape and therefore, selling it for $200,000 to you. You have found in the comparables that if the property was in great shape the property will be worth $350,000. After going through the property and assessing it with a contractor, you figured that it will cost about $80,000 to fix up the property. Paul, who is an investor and handyman himself, would be happy to buy the contract from you for $5,000, put in the work himself and flip it for $335,000 after he is done. In this case, Jill is happy to get the headache off her hands. You are happy for making $5,000 without putting any money into it. Paul is happy to get a great deal with potential great returns!

Finding the Buyer

Finding the buyer is very similar to finding the seller. Advertising, flyers and most importantly networking with other investors are great ways to find buyers. Since you have only a short period of time to have a buyer in place, it is very beneficial to record a list of potential buyers and their criteria for houses. You learn about it during your networking and replying to inquiries. Therefore, when the property comes across your hands that matches a few of the buyers on your lists, you can easily wholesale the deal to them with minimal time.

Pros and Cons of Wholesaling

As we have said before, for you to Make More and Work Less with real estate, you must put in the work first. With wholesaling, it is the best strategy for those with minimal capital. It generally takes about eight to ten total hours to negotiate a deal and have all the closings take place. However, wholesaling requires a lot of time building the buyers list and finding the motivated sellers. If you have the proper systems in place, finding buyers and sellers will get easier and easier, and wholesaling will require less and less work.

Rent – To –Own

The other strategy to make some money by finding paper is Rent-to-Own. Rent-to-Owning a property works very similarly to leasing a car. With a property that you have bought, you will find a tenant buyer for the property. Tenant buyers who are interested in this scenario are usually those who are unable to purchase a property now, be it poor credit or lack of a down payment, but would love to be a home owner. This is how you can help. After you have found the tenant buyer you will be renting the property to them with the option to purchase the property after a specified term, usually three to five years. You will require a fee as an option consideration which will go towards their future down payment for the house. This amount is usually about three month's rent, which is not enough to cover the down payment required to purchase the house in the future. Therefore, depending on the term that you have set, the remainder of the required down payment will be spread out throughout the term through rent as credit toward the future down payment at the end of the term if they choose to exercise the option. During the life of the term, your property will cashflow more due to the extra rent credit. You will also ensure that your tenant buyer is set up to succeed in exercising the option to buy the property. This means that they will be in contact with your team members, your mortgage broker and credit counselor. When the term is up and your tenant buyers have fulfilled all requirements to qualify for the property and decide to exercise the option to buy the property, the property will be sold to them at the current market price. A down payment for the property is not required as the rent credits and the option consideration at the beginning of the term will have made up for the required down payment. If the tenant buyers decide to not buy the property, then they will forfeit the option consideration and the rent credit that was accumulated. The advantages of this strategy is that you will have positive cashflow throughout the term of the option, have tenants that will treat the property like their home and also have buyers in place that will buy your property for the future price at the end of the term.

Rent-To-Own

Owner = You   Future Tenant Buyer
Current Price = $200,000   Down Payment = $11,000
                                                        (assuming 5%)
Future Price = $220,000   Down Payment Now = $3,600

Three-year term

Current Rent = $1,200
Rent Credit = $206/month
Total Rent + Credit = $1,406
Monthly Expense = $1,000
Total Cashflow = $406/month

End of term:

Tenant buyer buys property:
$220,000 - $3,600 - (36 months X $206) = $209,000

You collected:

$14,616 from three years of Cashflow plus $9,000 at close.

Net profit = $21,616 after lawyer fees (assuming ~$2,000)

Keys to Rent-to-Owning

To do Rent-to-Owning successfully, again a good system must be in place. Finding motivated sellers willing to sell their property below market value and finding tenant buyers for the property are the main factors. In the case of a rent-to-own, getting a property for below market value is not as important as wholesaling; however, it will increase your potential cashflow.

Pros and Cons of Rent-to-Own

Although the example given above shows you as the owner of the property, you can structure the rent-to-own with the original owner, where they still own the property, have you find a tenant buyer who will buy the property from you after an agreed term, and have taken possession after a previously agreed term. It is a method where you control the contracts and the house without ever putting any money in or be on title. This method known as Sandwich Lease Option is a great way to build your real estate portfolio without owning or paying for real estate. However, with rent-to-own, one must be great at handling problem situations with tenant buyers and managing the relationship with the original owners. This is because tenant buyers are generally going through a tough time and will require more hand-holding throughout the process.

Introduction to Wholesaling and Rent-to-Owning

Please keep in mind that this has been a very small discussion about wholesaling and Rent-to-Owning and that more is involved than what has been discussed. The purpose of this book as we have illustrated before is to open up your mind to different possibilities to Make More and Work Less. As an added bonus to you, we have included in this book a free report on the *Top 10 Questions and Answers About Real Estate That You MUST Know!* Please go to www.yourarea.ca, to claim your free report.

Do your due diligence, research and decide on your strategy, before taking action

Chapter - 8 -

Solve Problems, Make More

As we get further into the strategies of real estate, the ability to assess risk and manage risk gets more and more important. With Wholesaling and Rent-to-Own, you can potentially Make More and Work Less with minimal amount of your own money. You need mostly time. With the last two strategies: Buy-Fix and Flip and Buy and Hold, you may require both capital and time, but depending on your strengths, you have options to structure the following opportunities to fit your plans to Make More and Work Less.

Buy-Fix and Flip

The third strategy is Buy-Fix and Flip, which is where you will purchase a run-down property, fix it up cosmetically and then put it back into the market for sale. This strategy requires you to find properties that need work and also have people who can do renovations for you. For example, say you found a property that needs a lot of work: new floors, new kitchen, bathroom, new paint and new electrical. Due to its current condition, you were able to pick it up for $150,000. You know that if it was all fixed up, you would be able to sell the property for $300,000. After assessing the amount of work that needs to be done, you were given a quote of $60,000 that would bring the value of your property to the estimated $300,000. After all the repairs are completed and the initial costs to purchase plus closing costs you will make a profit of $67,000, usually in a span of four to six months.

Buy-Fix and Flipping is one of the best ways to generate large sums of capital with some of your own capital and/or time, and potentially be a great boost to your Make More and Work Less goal. An average person makes about $60,000 a year, working an average of 40 hours a week, about 2,080 hours a year. Using the example above, if renovations take about three months of time (most of it being done by others) and the advertising and selling of the property is also done by others, you have the potential to make $67,000 in four to six months without doing a lot except for managing the contractors and the real estate agent and putting the deal together. If you were to reinvest the profits of this property into another and then into another, you can potentially be making more money in one year than an average person makes in three to four years!

Buy-Fix-Flip

 →→ →
6 months

Current value = $150,000   Fixed up = $300,000
Renovation Cost = $60,000
Selling costs = $13,000
Lawyer fee = $2,000
Holding Cost = $8,000

Total = $233,000

Net Profit = $67,000

Keys to Buy-Fix and Flip

The keys to a Buy-Fix and Flip are very similar to that of a wholesale deal. However, you are now the investor, a wholesaler's buyer. Finding run-down, below market properties and assessing the value are just as important here as they are in a wholesale. You can work with wholesalers by telling them exactly what you are seeking in a property so they can do all the initial leg work for you. For a Buy-Fix and Flip, two other factors come into play: assessing renovating costs and having a great team of contractors at your disposal.

Assessing Renovating Costs

Determining how much renovations will cost could make or break any Buy-Fix and Flip deal. If you underestimate the cost, you may end up with a very bad deal. If you overestimate the cost, then you may have passed up on a great opportunity. It is very important not to take on a project where the property requires structural improvements. These projects are typically more costly and time consuming than a buy-fix and flip property that only requires cosmetic work. You are looking for properties that only need cosmetic improvements: new paint, new flooring, new bathrooms and kitchens. New roofs, windows, furnaces and water tanks also may be done, but be aware of these costs.

Before you close on a property, make sure you arrange for a couple of contractors that can give you a quote for what you want done. It is very important that you are clear and precise with what you want to see and to communicate to them what price range you are looking to spend. Very often, people underestimate the amount of time and money needed to renovate a property. Remember that if renovations are delayed, your holding costs increase. Another important factor is to be careful to not over renovate the property! What we mean by this is do not put in top quality items that do not increase the sale of the property. You do not want to be the most expensive property in the neighborhood. Therefore, renovate according to what the value of that neighborhood allows. Using the above example where the market value of the property after all is fixed is $300,000. The flooring and countertops to achieve that value according to other properties in the area are laminate floors and countertops. However, if properties in the area with granite countertops and hardwood flooring demand a price of $400,000, then spending the extra few thousand dollars is worth doing. In contrast, if all properties in the area will only sell at a maximum price of $310,000, regardless of hardwood flooring and granite countertops, then the extra cost may not be worth it.

Once you have a pretty firm idea as to what the cost of renovating will be, it is also very beneficial to add on another $5,000 to $10,000 in your estimate for miscellaneous situations. The contractor may need to delay due to issues at home or delivery date may be pushed due to weather. You never know what may happen and therefore, an extra cushion in cost always is recommended.

Team of Contractors

Through networking, building a database of contractors will be very helpful in these situations. If the relationship is built, you will trust them not to overcharge you and to provide high quality of work. Have a tile expert, a dry waller, a plumber, electrician and others in your database so that you can get the advice from professionals whom you trust, allowing you to make the best possible judgment on what you should be paying for the property and how much you should be allowing for renovations.

After a period of time, when the relationship is built and trust is formed, there may be opportunities for a joint venture with your contractors on future projects. Again, using the example from before, you got the property for $150,000. Your down payment of 20 percent is $30,000 of your own money. Your contractors quote you that materials and labor to renovate the property will be $60,000. If you trust your contractors and you have worked on previous projects together, you may want to include them in the deal. Ask if they would like to be a Joint Venture partner with you. You provided the project, the down payment and the work needed to get the property sold and they come in with the materials and labor. At the end, after the selling of the property, you will then split the profits 50/50 with your contractors. You are happy because instead of being out $113,000 to make $67,000, you are in the deal with $53,000, making $33,500. Your contractors are happy because they now can make an extra $33,500 for doing the same amount of work. In addition, because you and the contractors have a vested interest in the property, you want the best for the property. The contractors will do better work and work on time, knowing that if they do a poor job or are late, then it affects their profits in the end. The cost for labor may also be reduced due to the relationship and faster work. The contractor knows that you will not run off on them due to an agreement being made and that if the project works, more will come.

Pros and Cons with Buy-Fix and Flipping

Buy-Fix and Flip can generate great returns. However, if done poorly it can be very disastrous. Time and cost of a renovation project are two great factors that you need to assess. If you do not have the capital and time on your side, then buy-fix-and-flipping may be too risky. Similar to wholesaling, finding the properties with the profit potentials requires a lot of persistence and work. However, if you have the systems in place, do your due diligence and account for the time and costs correctly and conservatively, then Buy-Fix and Flipping is a great way to Make More and Work Less.

Introduction to Buy-Fix and Flipping

Please keep in mind that this is again a very small portion on buying-fixing and flipping properties. More is involved than what has been discussed. The purpose of this book as we have illustrated before is to open up your mind to different possibilities to Make More and Work Less. As an added bonus to you we have included in this book a free template to allow you to properly assess the numbers of a buy-fix and flip deal. Please go to www.makemoreworklessbook.com, to claim your free template.

Having a good team of contractors around you
will allow you to succeed.

Chapter - 9 -

Go Passive, Make More

After discussing the strategies of Wholesaling, Rent-to-Own and Buy-Fix and Flip, we now will mention our favorite strategy within our four pillars of financial foundation: Buy and Hold. We discussed in Chapter 2 about the concept of retirement, how the goal is to stop working and live off the saved money that you have earned throughout your life time. We challenged that thought by showing how the concept of retirement is outdated. If you love what you do, why must you stop? We would like to challenge that once again by asking, "What if you can structure a plan to create passive income that can last as long as you want it to last?" Isn't that the ultimate life for retirement? To have money coming in every month without doing much work at all? Isn't passive income the true answer to the question how to Make More and Work Less? It is because of passive income that we are so passionate about Buy and Hold.

Buy and Hold

Buy and hold is where you purchase a property, fix it up if need be, rent it and do so for five plus years or as long as you see fit. Every month throughout the years, you will be profiting after you have spent the costs of maintaining the property. These types of properties include single family homes, duplexes, 4-plexes, apartment buildings, commercial buildings and office buildings. At the end of the day, these properties bring in monthly passive income. They are cashflowing properties. Based on our experience for the purpose of providing assistance to those thinking of getting into real estate, single family homes that allow for separate basement suites are the best way to start. We believe it is the first step for any real estate investor.

If you have a little bit of capital or have access to funds, purchasing a cashflow property is a great way to start. It allows you to learn many facets of the industry and at the same time, acquire an asset that will open a lot of opportunities down the road.

Buy-Hold

Income: Main Rent = $1,100
                  Basement Rent = $850

Expenses: Mortgage = $850/month
                  Property Tax = $150/month
                  Insurance = $50/month
                  Miscellaneous = $200/month

Total Cashflow per month = Income - Expense = $700

Total Cashflow after five years = $42,000

As we mentioned before, there are many types of cashflowing properties. The overall concept is the same when assessing your numbers and analyzing the property. For the purposes of this book, we will focus on single family homes that allow for separate basement suites as shown in the example above.

The Strategy for your Plan

In the example above, we have a cashflow per month of $700. That is $700 a month extra that you normally would not have had. You can use the cashflow to set up more insurance, buy more gold, pay off debt, pay down the mortgage faster or accumulate it for more real estate. After five years, you have accumulated $42,000 in total cashflow, equity built up and the likely appreciation of the property itself. You can refinance the property and use the combined funds to purchase another one or two properties. You can reinvest the profits over and over again and before long, you will have built an empire of properties just because of starting with one. Of course, that is the ideal plan and to see that plan become a reality, it will require work and persistence at the beginning. As you gain more and more experience, it will get easier and faster. Life really could be like the game of monopoly!

Keys to Buy and Hold

For a buy and hold to succeed, there are three important key factors: finding a cash flowing property, finding the tenants and lastly maintaining the cashflow property.

Finding the Right Cashflowing Property

Finding the right cashflow property requires some research and analysis on your part. You can have your agent set up searches and send you what comes up but ultimately, it is you that will need to determine if the property is good as a cashflow property or not. Is the property in a good rental area? Are there a lot of problems in that neighborhood? What kind of rents can I expect in this area? Is the property a multi-unit building? Does it have separate up and down suites? Can it become separate suites? Are there separate entrances? Is there a garage that you can rent as well? How much renovation is needed to be done? These are all questions that you need to consider when looking at an investment property. Note that you can also combine the buy-fix-flip scenario with buy and hold where after you do all the renovations and you now have a cashflow property where you rent it for the long term.

Finding these properties like all the other types of properties will require a keen eye on listings, newspapers, networking events, referrals, advertising and many other techniques.

Keep in mind that what you will accept is what determines a good cashflow deal for you. Is $200 cashflow good? $400? How about $800? Maybe a single rental house fits your needs more than an up and down suite. Can you handle the risk of vacancy? How much down payment do you want to put down to create higher cashflow? It all comes down to your comfort level and risk tolerance.

Finding the Right Tenants

Finding the right tenants is very important. You want to be able to trust that the people you put into the property will not damage the property and will pay their rent. A great way of screening tenants is with an application form before you spend time showing the potential tenants the property. In the application, you should have required information, such as current job, current home, work references, previous landlord references and credit checks. People who have something to hide or know that they will not get good feedback from their reference will usually not fill out the application completely or at all. This gives you the indication they are not serious enough to rent your place and/or probably not qualified either.

After qualifying the potential tenant with their application form, set up a viewing with them at the property. Ask good questions and take note as to what they are like. Do they like pets? Do they smoke? What is their work schedule like? Knowing as much about them will allow you to get a better feel as to what type of renter they will be. How are they dressed? Are they drunk? Is their car messy? The answer to these questions and much more can indicate to you how well they treat their own things, let alone your property. In the end you also want to trust your instincts. How do you feel about this potential renter? After seeing multiple applicants, you will get into a zone and be able to screen tenants with ease. If on occasion you stumble on a trouble tenant, don't be discouraged, learn from it and find a better one.

Maintaining the Property

Finding the perfect tenant also requires nurturing to keep the tenant a perfect tenant and also to keep the tenant renting from you. To do so, you must treat the tenant well and put yourself in their shoes. Build rapport with the tenant so that they feel special being your tenant. Address their needs with care and in a timely manner so that they know that you have their best interest in mind. You must also show them what their responsibilities are, so that they know what you expect of them. Are they responsible for lawn work or snow shoveling? Are they expected to change light bulbs? Have all documentation signed and copied so that they know what they agreed to do.

Having your tenants feel special renting from you will pay back in strides. Whether it is from them referring other renters to you, them wanting to renew or simply them watching out for you by telling you problems with the other tenants and what is going on with your properties. When you give possession of the unit to your tenant, have a welcome basket of things they will need to move in or things that they enjoy (hence getting to know them). Offering Christmas gifts or a simple "Happy Birthday" will go a long way to making them feel that you care and are happy to have them as your renters. If you are in doubt of your abilities to manage the property, you can always hire a property manager to do so for you. Once you have a system set for maintaining your properties and tenants, you will soon see that you will Make More and Work Less.

Live in your Home for FREE!

There are a lot of people out there that tell us, "Well we really want to have a cashflow property, but at the same time, we also need to get something for ourselves to live in, so we don't think we can do both at the moment." To that we tell them, "but, you can do both!" We understand that everyone's situation is different and everyone's needs and tolerance are different, but if you are open minded and willing to try nontraditional strategies, then you are able to have both your own home AND a cashflow property.

Say for instance, you are looking for your own home and a cashflowing property. You are thinking that within three to five years, you will probably move on to a bigger or nicer place. At the moment, you only can afford something smaller with less monthly payments. Why not look for a cashflow property and live in it yourself, whether it is on the main floor or basement floor and rent the other level out to someone else. If done strategically you can essentially live in your own home for FREE! After three to five years, you can more easily afford the bigger and nicer home that you wanted, with the savings you had from living for "free". After you move out and into your new home, you can now rent the floor you were living in and maintain a cashflow property.

For example, you purchase an up and down duplex for $300,000. The monthly mortgage payments are $1,400, property tax is $250/month and insurance for the house is $75/month. Total monthly expense is $1,725. As a complete separate suite, you know you can rent the bottom unit for about $1,600 a month. Therefore, you will be living in your own home almost for FREE! After five years, you will have saved $96,000 ($1,600 X 60 months) that you would have paid originally, an equity pay down of about $25,000 and a potential appreciation of about $30,000. Let's say you have a better job now and can support a mortgage on your own and found your dream home for $400,000. A down payment on your new home may be around $80,000 for a conventional mortgage. From the money, you saved and the value of the house you currently own, you have access to about $150,000. After the down payment for your new home you still have $70,000 left over! With the remaining funds, you can purchase another up and down duplex similar to the one you had before and let that bring in passive income of about $1,500/month. But wait! You still have the first up and down duplex that you lived in, which you have now rented out fully and is also cashflowing $1,500/month. With the added cashflow from both properties you can essentially be living in your new home for FREE too! As you can see, there are many possibilities for what you can do with real estate and how you can Make More and Work Less. This is just one scenario of what one can do.

Pros and Cons with Buy and Hold

As we have illustrated above, the advantages of a buy and hold property, if structured properly are endless. You can own an asset, have someone pay it down, access more funds and do it all over again. The downside is the time and work needed to manage the property. This can be mitigated by approving great tenants and hiring a property manager to manage the property for you. As long as you factor in the cost of the manager and you can still get positive cashflow, then your investment is in good hands.

Introduction to Buy and Hold

Once again, we want to remind you that this is a small sampling of what buy and holding cashflow properties is all about. There are a lot more items to explore than what has been discussed. The purpose of this book as we have illustrated before is to open up your mind to different possibilities to Make More and Work Less. To thank you for reading this far, we would like to give you a GIANT bonus! Also included in this book are 3 free chapters of our book *Make More Work Less With CASHFLOW Properties: The Step by Step Keys to Analyzing, Acquiring and Maintaining Cashflow Properties.*

Please go to www.makemoreworklessbook.com, to claim your bonus.

Once you have all the right pieces together:
finding, acquiring and maintaining
cashflow properties are simple.

Chapter - 10 -

Think Different, Make More

The purpose of this book is to open your mind to multiple vehicles you can explore, implement and set up to Make More and Work Less in your own way. These are by no means guaranteed methods and that success is a given. Success is governed by mindset as discussed in the first chapter and your willingness to take action. Nothing will happen if you don't do anything with the knowledge you have learned. One must put a plan in place and take the steps to see it through to completion.

Plan

Planning is a key component to success. Imagine what it would be like if someone told you to visit a place you've never seen and you had no access to a map. You would feel lost wouldn't you? It's the same thing as planning to be successful without having a way to get there.

Let's say you want to have one cashflowing property in two months. What must you do to get there? How many offers do you have to make? How many places do you have to see? How many calls do you have to make? Just work backwards from your goals and you will have a plan. Remember, as George S. Patton once said, "A good plan violently executed now is better than a perfect plan executed next week." So start with a plan and adjust it as you move along.

Set yearly, monthly and daily goals and activities. Review your goals every day and plan what you want to accomplish the next day. This will allow you to wake up ready to go! You will have a plan as to what you need to do and when you need to finish it.

Remember back in school when the teacher tells you that you'll have a test on the 15th? When do you study? The 13th? The 14th? The morning of the 15th? What happens when the teacher tells you that the test is postponed until the 20th? When would you study then? If you were to plan ahead and set aside some time every day to review and study the material, would you ever be anxious as to when the test will be? Would you ever need to pull an all nighter to study for the test last minute? Having a plan in place will allow you to focus and manage your energy and time. You will no longer be wasting time thinking of what you need to do or if you have forgotten anything.

Setting goals allow you to strive for something. While goals are great, many goals are unattained mainly because people are not capable of setting goals correctly. People set goals that are too unachievable in the time period they want. Their goals can also be too vague. They could have no timeline. Let's look at these a little more closely and find out how we can avoid these mistakes.

If the goal is too grand, the possibility of failure is great. For example, if your goal for this year is to have 10 cashflow properties when you don't have any properties or knowledge at all, then the chances of success are very slim. However if you were to set three levels of goals at: level 1- one property, level 2- five properties, and level 3- 10 properties, then the chances of you reaching one or all of your goals would be higher. On top of that, each time you reach a goal, you will be more motivated to reach the next level.

If a goal is too vague, then one will never know if the goal is reached or not. For example, if one were to say: "I want an investment" well what does that mean? What kind? How many? Does buying one silver coin count? Are you going into stocks? Real Estate? However, if one were to say "I want a cashflowing single family property to bring in a positive cashflow of at least $500 monthly by April next year," then, we know exactly what you want and when you will achieve that goal.

Finally if a goal has no timeline, then it will never get done. Think back to the tests that your teachers gave you. If they never told you a date, would you ever have studied for an undisclosed date? Probably not. Without a date, goals tend to be pushed aside and forgotten. The power of having dates will also allow you to work backward and set mini goals and dates for you to meet your goals. For example, if your goal is to have 10 cashflowing properties by the end of the year, then you may have a goal of attaining five in six months. When six months comes around and you have five properties, then you know that you are on track to meet your annual goal. This way you can break down your plan into five-year goals, two-year goals, nine-month goals, monthly and daily goals.

After setting your goals, you will find that planning and strategizing your actions become easier and easier. This may be an overwhelming task to begin with and therefore we highly recommend you seek the help of a coach or a mentor.

Setting goals and achieving them are a vital part of success. But, this is not a goal-setting book, so we will not go into more detail on how to set or achieve goals. However, our mentor and friend Raymond Aaron has written a bestselling hardcover book *Double Your Income Doing What You Love*, recognized as the world's No. 1 authority on goal achievement. In fact, on the back cover, there are testimonials from giant celebrities who use his program. One such testimonial is by Jack Canfield, the co-creator of the *Chicken Soup For The Soul* series of books. Here is his testimonial: *"The reason I personally chose to use this amazing system for myself and for my company is that, bluntly stated, it is the most powerful system ever created."* By special arrangement, we have permission to allow you, our dear reader, to own a copy of Mr. Aaron's book for free and you can get it by instant download simply by going to his website, www.aaron.com.

What if I Have no Time and or Money to Save or Invest?

If you contribute absolutely nothing you will get nothing. If you truly want to Make More and Work Less, then you must do something to make it happen. Whether it is to talk to an adviser, an insurance broker or a real estate agent, you must first start the ball rolling. The funny thing about time is, if you write down what you want to do and you schedule it ahead of time, you will find that you will be able to make the time to do the things you want to do. The key word here is 'WANT'. How badly do you want to Make More and Work Less? How important is your financial future?

During the section about Buy-Fix-and-Flips, we have mentioned the possibility of joint venturing with your contractors. What is stopping you from joint venturing with a money partner or another investor? For example, if you have money but no time, seek out real estate investors that can do all the work for you, utilizing the strategies discussed before and provide you with a return that allows your money to grow. Likewise, if you have no money, then partner with those who have money and you do all the work. As long as you keep in mind the concepts of "how can I add value to them," you will find the partners needed to succeed.

Manage your time effectively and prioritize what you want to get done. There are no secrets to time management. It comes down to committing to what you want to achieve and just doing it. Write down your goals and what you need to do to achieve them. Once you know what you need to do, schedule those items into your calendar and stick to it. Set aside 20 minutes a day or one hour a week. Even if it isn't a lot, it is progressing toward reaching your goals. There are great books that will help you with time management. We recommend the *4-Hour Work Week* by Timothy Ferris.

Does my Credit Affect on What I Can Do?

The ability to qualify and access credit may be very important in your quest to Make More and Work Less. To set up a banking system with insurance, get into exempt markets, invest in gold and silver, build a business with network marketing and various strategies of real estate, such as wholesaling and rent-to-own, having access to credit may not be necessary as long as you have some cash.

With regards to insurance, exempt markets, commodities and network marketing, it really comes down to where you want to put your money. If you are currently contributing to a savings account, maybe it would be more advantageous to contribute a portion of that into an insurance policy that can create a banking system for you. If you are already contributing money into a government supported retirement plan, such as mutual funds in a register savings plans or tax free savings plan, it would grow even faster if you contributed some of those funds into an exempt market or silver instead. These are funds that you would have been using for savings or retirement anyway, why not put it to better use?

Even in certain situations where credit is normally essential, such as buy-fix and flipping properties or holding cashflowing properties can be done without accessing your own credit. Joint ventures with other people and have them qualify for mortgages or loans while you do all the work. That way, you can save some of your qualifying power for projects that need to qualify for quick loans if you do not have anyone in place, while providing your JV partner with more peace of mind, knowing that they are on title.

Knowing your credit score is very important. This will allow you to know if you are in good standing with lenders and banks. Your ability to qualify for a loan is related to how high your credit score is. Your credit score is based on your ability to service debt. Are you able to handle debt? Do you pay your bills on time? Are your credit cards maxed out? Does the debt service ratio of the rental property you are picking up meet the requirements? Depending on the lender, ratios vary. Basically, for a rental, they would like to know if the rent will cover all the expenses. Likewise, they also will like to know if you are able to cover all the expenses of your everyday life on top of the rental property if rent is not coming in. If you have good credit, there are always opportunities to increase its standing with strategic credit management. To do so, we recommend that you have another team member, a credit expert, who understands the rules and regulations and can give you tips as to how you can increase your credit score. Likewise, if you have poor credit or are experiencing debt issues, a credit manager or debt counselor will have the expertise to help you get out of debt quickly and build up your credit again. Your mortgage broker should also know the tricks of the trade to qualify if needed. Therefore, discussions with your broker are very important.

Regardless of whether you need good credit or not, to implement a strategy to Make More and Work Less, it is always beneficial to know what your credit situation is and how to make it better.

Build a Team

There is no way you can do everything yourself and no way you can invest in every great deal that you find. So build a team of professionals and friends that can be there for you. A mortgage broker, a real estate agent, an exempt market specialist, an insurance broker, financial adviser (independent of a banking institution), real estate investors, contractors, and, most importantly, a coach are all intricate members of your team.

Coach

A coach is one of the most vital team members you can have. He or she should be someone who is currently doing what you want to do. If he or she has done it in the past and is not currently doing it, then they may not be up to date on how the market works. A coach is vital in that he or she can help you avoid the mistakes that he or she has made and guide you in a way to faster success than if you had stumbled around blind. Remember back in the chapter on mindset? As you are learning about new ways to Make More and Work Less, there will always be things that you don't know. A coach can point this out for you and show you things that may cause you problems later.

Coaches are also able to show you where you can go. They can show you what may have been impossible in your mind and make it possible. Coaches should be experienced, accountable, motivational and inspirational. They should have your best interest in mind. Bouncing off all decisions with your coach will ensure less issues in your path forward.

Just like how athletes have a nutrition coach, a game coach and a mental coach, it is to your advantage to have multiple coaches for the multiple aspects of your life.

In Closing

After looking deeper into our current retirement plans, we hope that we all agree that the concept is outdated and needs to be rethought. By looking at how our Four Pillars of Financial Foundation: Insurance, Land, Commodities and Real Estate, can provide the safety and assurance of a comfortable financial future and potentially a financial future that continues to grow, we hope that we have opened your mind to be accepting of new and nontraditional ways of financial planning and investing.

Planning and setting up for a fulfilling financial future is like riding a bike. You may be scared to explore and try it, but that is what your coach is for – to guide you along the way and help you avoid potential pitfalls and tell you what to expect. You may stumble and fall at times, but your coach and power team will be there to pick you up and together, you will learn from the mistakes that caused you to stumble. With the right determination and will, you will soar. You will celebrate the success of your work and time and Make More while you Work Less.

**With determination and will,
success will be close behind.**

- FINAL THOUGHTS -

Thank you for taking the time to read our book. We have put a lot of effort into this to make it as straightforward and easily understood as a guideline on how to Make More and Work Less. We felt that by adding practical tips, we could give you the keys to the problems you could encounter.

By now, you have already learned about the following:

1) Mindset
2) Our Pillars of Financial Foundation
3) Taking Action and the Importance of Coaching

You might be thinking, "I read your book, what's next?" Well, that's a valid question. We've found all too often that a book, while comprehensive, sometimes leaves us with some questions we want answered. To help you move even further along, we have compiled a collection of videos from the best authorities in the market to help you. The members of our power team and our coaches have answered the most commonly asked questions in their field to add value for our treasured readers.

For more information on this, please visit www.yourarea.ca. If you have any questions you wish to have answered regarding this book, please feel free to e-mail us at makemoreworklessquestion@yourarea.ca. Please note that we get plenty of questions and e-mails daily, but we will do our best to answer your questions.

We will now leave you with one last quote from Dr. Phil. "Anyone can do something when they WANT to do it. Really successful people do things when they don't want to do it." So go out there and reach your dreams!

Recommended Book List

MINDSET
Change your mind Change your Results – Shawn Shewchuk
The Magic of Thinking Big – David Schwartz
Think and Grow Rich – Napoleon Hill
Who Moved My Cheese – Spencer Johnson

TIME MANAGEMENT
The Four Hour Work Week – Tim Ferriss

GOAL SETTING
Double Your Income Doing What You Love – Raymond Aaron

RELATIONSHIP BUILDING
How to Win Friends and Influence People – Dale Carnegie
Crucial Confrontations – Kerry Patterson, Joseph Grenny, Ron McMillan, Al Switzler
Crucial Conversations – Kerry Patterson, Joseph Grenny, Ron McMillan, Al Switzler

INSURANCE
Becoming your Own Banker - R. Nelson Nash
Building your Warehouse of Wealth - R. Nelson Nash
The Banker's Secret by Glen Zacher and Jayson Lowe of McGuire Financial

COMMODITIES
Guide to Investing in Gold and Silver – Michael Maloney
The Dollar Crisis – Richard Duncan

REAL ESTATE/BUSINESS
Rich Dad Poor Dad – Robert Kiyosaki
Cashflow Quadrant – Robert Kiyosaki
Trump: Strategies for Real Estate – George Ross
Business Lessons from JT Foxx – JT Foxx

Made in the USA
Charleston, SC
11 April 2015